W9-AGR-479

CONTRIBUTORS AND CONSULTANTS

HALL BARTLETT, *Ed.D., Citizenship Education Project, Teachers College, Columbia University; Author*

WALT DISNEY, *Motion Picture and Television Producer*

EVELYN MILLIS DUVALL, *Ph.D., Author and Consultant on Family Life; Authority on Child Development*

EDNA E. EISEN, *Ph.D., Professor of Geography, Kent State University*

J. ALLEN HYNEK, *Ph.D., Associate Director, Smithsonian Astrophysical Observatory*

LELAND B. JACOBS, *Ph.D., Professor of Education, Teachers College, Columbia University*

ELEANOR M. JOHNSON, *M.A., Director of Elementary School Services, Graduate Division, Wesleyan University*

HERBERT A. LANDRY, *M.S., Ph.D., Director, Bureau of Educational Program Research and Statistics, New York City Public Schools*

MILTON LEVINE, *M.D., Associate Professor of Pediatrics, New York Hospital*

WILLY LEY, *Professor of Science, Fairleigh Dickinson University; Rocket Expert and Author*

NORMAN LLOYD, *M.A., Teacher of Literature and Materials of Music, Juilliard School of Music*

LENOX R. LOHR, *M.E., D.Eng., D.Sc., President, Museum of Science and Industry, Chicago*

WILL C. McKERN, *D.S., Former Director, Milwaukee Public Museum; Anthropologist*

RICHARD A. MARTIN, *B.S., Curator, N. W. Harris Public School Extension, Chicago Natural History Museum*

MAURICE PATE, *Executive Director, United Nations Children's Fund (UNICEF)*

NORMAN VINCENT PEALE, *D.D., LL.D., Litt.D., LH.D.; Minister, Marble Collegiate Church, New York; Author*

RUTHERFORD PLATT, *B.A., Member of Two North Pole Expeditions with Admiral MacMillan; Author of Nature Books*

ILLA PODENDORF, *M.S., Teacher of Science, University of Chicago Laboratory Schools; Author of Science Books*

MARY M. REED, *Ph.D., Supervisor of Little Golden Books; Formerly of Teachers College, Columbia University*

JOHN R. SAUNDERS, *M.A., Chairman, Department of Public Instruction, American Museum of Natural History*

GLENN T. SEABORG, *Ph.D., LL.D., D.Sc., Chancellor and Professor of Chemistry, University of California, Berkeley; Associate Director, University of California Radiation Laboratory; Co-winner of Nobel Prize for Chemistry, 1951*

LOUIS SHORES, *Ph.D., Dean of the Library School, Florida State University; Author and Authority on Reference Materials*

NILA BANTON SMITH, *Ph.B., Ph.D., Professor of Education and Director of The Reading Institute, New York University*

BRYAN SWAN, *M.S., Teacher of Physical Science, University of Chicago Laboratory Schools; Author*

SAMUEL TERRIEN, *S.T.M., Th.D., Auburn Professor of the Old Testament, Union Theological Seminary*

JESSIE TODD, *M.A., Formerly of the Art Department, University of Chicago; Art Lecturer; Contributor to Art Magazines*

LLOYD B. URDAL, *Ph.D., Assistant Professor, School of Education, State College of Washington*

JANE WERNER WATSON, *B.A., Editor and Author of More Than a Hundred Golden Books*

WILLIAM S. WEICHERT, *M.S., Supervisor of Science, Oakland (Calif.) Public Schools*

PAUL A. WITTY, *Ph.D., Professor of Education, Northwestern University; Specialist on Gifted Children*

STAFF

ROBERT D. BEZUCHA, *Project Director;* NORMAN F. GUESS, *Editorial Director;* R. JAMES ERTEL, *Managing Editor;* PAULINE NORTON, *Assistant Project Director;* ALICE F. MARTIN, *Associate Editor. Staff Editors:* GENEVIEVE CURLEY, JOAN FALK, HESTER GELB, RICHARD D. HARKINS.

THE GOLDEN BOOK ENCYCLOPEDIA

VOLUME XVI—WALES TO ZOOS; INDEX

In Sixteen Accurate, Fact-filled Volumes Dramatically Illustrated
with More Than 6,000 Color Pictures

THE ONLY ENCYCLOPEDIA FOR YOUNG GRADE-SCHOOL CHILDREN

ACCURATE AND AUTHORITATIVE

ENTERTAININGLY WRITTEN AND ILLUSTRATED TO
MAKE LEARNING AN ADVENTURE

by Bertha Morris Parker

Formerly of the Laboratory Schools, University of Chicago
Research Associate, Chicago Natural History Museum

GOLDEN PRESS · NEW YORK

The letter W is one of the five letters that can be traced back to a single letter in the Phoenician alphabet (Y). The Greeks wrote it in two ways (Ϝ Υ). The Romans left off the tail of Y and wrote the letter in this way: V. The letter stood for two sounds—the sound of W in way and the sound of oo in boot. After a while the Romans began pronouncing the letter as we do our V. They needed another letter for the W sound. To get one they put two V's together.

W stands for only one sound—the sound it has in we. In wren, two, answer, and many other words it is silent.

WALES The country of Wales fills a mountainous, rainy peninsula stretching westward from England. About 675 years ago, England's King Edward I gained control of Wales. He called his first son the Prince of Wales. Giving that title to the eldest son of a ruler of England and Wales became a custom. England, Wales, Scotland, and Northern Ireland now are parts of the country of Britain. In 1952 Queen Elizabeth II became Britain's ruler. In 1958 her young son Charles was given the title Prince of Wales. The Welsh people elect some of the members of the British Parliament. It meets in Britain's great capital—London, England.

More than two-thirds of the people of Wales live in or near the narrow lowland along its southern coast. Most of the others live in or near the lowland strip that stretches along its northern coast.

Not far from the southern coast there are outcrops of good coal in the slopes of the valleys of southward flowing streams. Many miners live in small stone houses in long, narrow villages in the valleys. Small railroads carry coal to the coast to meet iron ore, tin, zinc, and copper brought by ocean ships. In Swansea and other places thousands of Welsh work in great mills that make metal goods of many kinds.

The mountainous part of Wales is thinly settled. There is little crop land. But on slopes in mountain valleys there is much grassland. Most farmers there raise cattle or sheep. No railroad crosses mountainous central Wales to connect the north and south lowlands. One part of the University of Wales is near the north coast, another is near the west coast. The people love harp music and old songs in the Welsh language. Summer music festivals bring many visitors to Wales. (See ELIZABETH II; ENGLAND; GREAT BRITAIN; UNITED KINGDOM.)

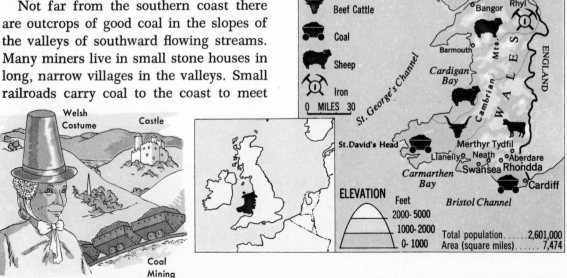

Welsh Costume

Castle

Coal Mining

Dairying

Beef Cattle

Coal

Sheep

Iron

0 MILES 30

IRISH SEA

Angelsey
Bangor
Rhyl
Barmouth
Cardigan Bay
St. George's Channel
Cambrian Mts.
WALES
ENGLAND
St. David's Head
Merthyr Tydfil
Llanelly
Neath
Aberdare
Carmarthen Bay
Swansea
Rhondda
Cardiff
Bristol Channel

ELEVATION
Feet
2000-5000
1000-2000
0-1000

Total population......2,601,000
Area (square miles)......7,474

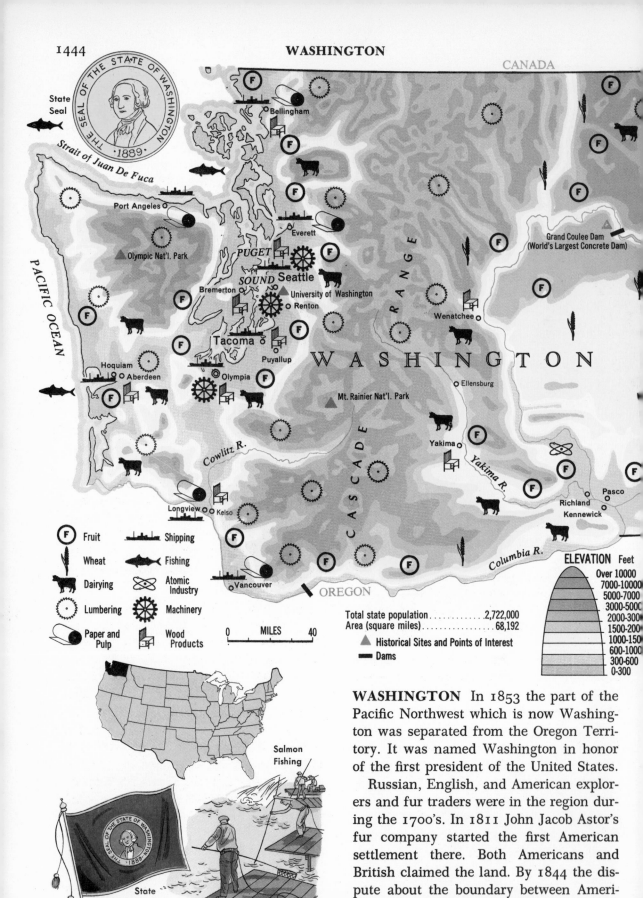

State Seal

THE SEAL OF THE STATE OF WASHINGTON · 1889 ·

Strait of Juan De Fuca

CANADA

PACIFIC OCEAN

Bellingham

Port Angeles

Olympic Nat'l. Park

Everett

PUGET

SOUND Seattle

Bremerton

University of Washington

Renton

Tacoma

Puyallup

Hoquiam
Aberdeen

Olympia

Cowlitz R.

C A S C A D E

R A N G E

W A S H I N G T O N

Wenatchee

Ellensburg

Mt. Rainier Nat'l. Park

Yakima

Yakima R.

Grand Coulee Dam
(World's Largest Concrete Dam)

Pasco
Richland
Kennewick

Longview Kelso

Vancouver

Columbia R.

OREGON

ELEVATION Feet

Over 10000
7000-10000
5000-7000
3000-5000
2000-300
1500-200
1000-150
600-1000
300-600
0-300

Legend:
- F Fruit
- Wheat
- Dairying
- Lumbering
- Paper and Pulp
- Shipping
- Fishing
- Atomic Industry
- Machinery
- Wood Products

0 MILES 40

Total state population............2,722,000
Area (square miles)................68,192
▲ Historical Sites and Points of Interest
▬ Dams

Salmon Fishing

State Flag

WASHINGTON In 1853 the part of the Pacific Northwest which is now Washington was separated from the Oregon Territory. It was named Washington in honor of the first president of the United States.

Russian, English, and American explorers and fur traders were in the region during the 1700's. In 1811 John Jacob Astor's fur company started the first American settlement there. Both Americans and British claimed the land. By 1844 the dispute about the boundary between American and British territory became bitter.

Mountain Scenery

Spokane R.

Spokane

IDAHO

Totem Pole

State Flower: Coast Rhododendron

nake R.

Walla

State Capitol

Fishing and mining increased, too. In 1889 Washington became the 42nd state.

Trade with the Far East and Alaska became important. Seattle was the nearest American port to these places. The Alaskan gold rush of 1897-1898 brought people and business to the state. When lands in the dry region east of the Cascade Mountains were irrigated, farming increased. Spokane became a trade center.

Washington has continued to grow. It is the most thickly populated state in the Pacific Northwest. The Puget Sound ports handle much shipping. One of the biggest changes has been the rapid growth of the aluminum and aircraft industries. Grand Coulee and other dams supply water for irrigation and electric power. New irrigation has added thousands of acres to the farmlands. Dairying is important. Orchards still furnish fine apples and other fruits. Although no longer first, Washington's forests supply much timber.

Only a little over 100 years ago Seattle was a small port and sawmill town on a sheltered bay off of Puget Sound. The settlers called the little village New York Alki. The Indian word "alki" means "by and by." Seattle is the "New York" of the Pacific Northwest. It is its largest city, with about half a million people. Ships from many parts of the world come to its docks. From its airport airplanes go to such places as Asia and Alaska.

From the top-floor windows of one of Seattle's fine hotels one sees the tall business buildings of the downtown section, the heavy traffic on the wide streets, and the beautiful homes near the shores of Lake Washington. One sees, too, factory smokestacks, and ships coming into the harbor. If the skies are clear, the cone-shaped peak of Mt. Rainier looms up.

West of Puget Sound is Olympic National Park. It is a region of forests, mountains, glaciers, and flower-covered meadows. No wonder Washington is called the "Switzerland of America."

The cry "54-40 or fight" swept the country. It meant that the United States claimed the land to 54°40′ north latitude. The 49th parallel finally became the boundary.

Sailing ships and stagecoaches brought settlers to Washington. Cattlemen took over the grazing ranges in eastern Washington. When a railroad was completed across the territory in 1887, settlement increased. Most of the open range disappeared. Wheat fields and fruit orchards began to flourish. Douglas fir trees and other giants of the rain forests on the western slopes of the Coast Ranges supplied timber for a booming lumber industry.

Booker could remember slave markets.

WASHINGTON, BOOKER T. (1856-1915)

In a book called *Up from Slavery*, Booker T. Washington tells the story of his life. The story is a wonderful one. Born a slave, Washington became a great leader. He traveled all over the world telling about the problems of the Negro. He probably did as much as any person in history to bring about a better understanding of his race.

Booker T. Washington was born on a plantation in Virginia. He was only a boy when all the slaves were freed at the end of the War between the States. First he worked in a salt mine and then in a coal mine. At night he studied. When he was old enough, he hitchhiked his way to Hampton Institute, a famous school for Negroes in Hampton, Va. He worked as a janitor to earn his way through the school and graduated in 1875. He was so good a student that, soon after he graduated, he was asked to teach there.

In 1881 the people of Tuskegee, Ala., asked Washington to come to Tuskegee and found a new school for Negroes. He went. Classes at first were held in a church and an old shanty. Washington was the only teacher. There were only about 40 students. The school grew fast. It became Tuskegee Institute. When Washington died, it had 101 buildings and thousands of acres of land. More important, it had 200 teachers and 1,500 students! (See EMANCIPATION PROCLAMATION; SLAVERY.)

WASHINGTON, GEORGE (1732-1799)

In 1747 Lawrence Washington asked his 15-year-old half brother to come live with him in his beautiful home called Mount Vernon. The half brother was George Washington. Lawrence had always liked George, and he knew that George would be a big help in running his plantation.

No one knows very much about Washington's early boyhood. The story of his cutting down the cherry tree and other such stories were probably made up. But of course some things are known.

George Washington was born on a farm called Wakefield in Virginia on Feb. 22, 1732. Odd as it seems, the calendar said the day Washington was born was Feb. 11.

George Washington

About 20 years later the calendar was changed. All dates in the records were moved up 11 days.

George's father was Augustine Washington. His mother was Mary Ball Washington. He had two older half brothers, Lawrence and Augustine. There were five children younger than he — three boys and two girls. George was tall and strong. He was good at games. His life was probably much like the life of all children of his time. When he was 11, his father died.

There was not much chance for George to go to school. His best chance was when he visited his half brother Augustine. Near Augustine's plantation was a good school.

Wakefield was Washington's birthplace.

Life at Mount Vernon with Lawrence was pleasant. For fun there were fox hunts and dances. There was swimming, too, in the Potomac River that flowed past the plantation. From the plantation owners he met, George learned the manners of a gentleman. Lord Fairfax, a neighbor, was interested in him and taught him a great deal.

But George liked work, too. Lord Fairfax hired him to do some surveying and was pleased with the work. Gradually George had more to do with running his half brother's plantation, for Lawrence became ill. When Lawrence took a sea voyage for his health, George went with him. On the trip both of them had smallpox. They recovered from it, but shortly after returning home Lawrence died. He left beautiful Mount Vernon to George.

Although Washington and his neighbors had beautiful homes, there was still fron-

Mt. Vernon became Washington's home.

tier land a little way to the west. The French threatened to take over some of the western territory that England claimed. For more than three years Washington was away from Mount Vernon, fighting against the French much of the time. He earned the reputation of being very brave.

When the war with the French was over, Washington married Martha Custis, a widow with two children. Soon he was elected to be a burgess and help govern Virginia. Before long he was taking part in debates about how England was governing the colonies. When England sent troops to Boston to see that some new taxes were paid, Washington was angry. "This is an act of tyranny," he said. He now agreed with

As a young man he learned how to survey land.

many others that it was time for the colonies to break away from England. He was ready to do his share in a war.

His share turned out to be a very big one. He was chosen to be the commander in chief of the American army. Soon afterward the Declaration of Independence was signed, and the war was on in earnest.

Washington's army was small. There was little money to pay the soldiers or to buy them the clothing and the arms they needed. Often they were ragged and hungry. At times it looked as if the colonies would surely lose. Only Washington's cleverness and his willingness to spend his own money kept the war going. Once

Washington and his soldiers crossed the Delaware.

in a while his men won a victory. Even when they lost, they made the British pay a high price for winning.

Help from France, largely from Lafayette, finally brought a turn in the war. In 1783 it was over and a new nation had been born—the United States of America.

Washington now wanted to be a gentleman farmer again. But the young nation did not get off to a good start. There was much quarreling among different sections. Someone well liked by everybody was needed as a leader. Of course, the one best fitted for being leader was George Washington. There was talk of making him king. But finally he was made president.

The choice of Washington as the leader of the new country was a wise one. Not only by his fighting but also by his work

Washington spent a hard winter at Valley Forge.

as president, Washington earned the right to be called the father of his country.

For eight years he guided the young nation. He had some excellent helpers. In his first cabinet Thomas Jefferson was secretary of state and Alexander Hamilton was secretary of the treasury.

During the Revolutionary War the 13 colonies had acted like 13 separate little nations. Washington helped build them into one strong nation. While he was president three new states were added—Vermont, Kentucky, and Tennessee.

One of Washington's important acts was to establish a mint for coining money. Another was to put down a revolt of some farmers in Pennsylvania. These farmers refused to pay a tax on liquor they made.

Washington said goodbye to his soldiers.

Washington kept the United States out of trouble with England. When a war began between France and England, some Americans wanted to help France by capturing British merchant ships. Washington would not allow it.

It was a happy day for Washington when he could turn over the work of governing to John Adams and go back to Mount Vernon. Two years later he died from a cold he caught riding over his plantation. One of his officers called Washington "First in war, first in peace, and first in the hearts of his countrymen." Almost everyone agreed.

WASHINGTON, D.C. This city, the capital of the United States, was named for George Washington, the first president of the United States. Washington chose the location for the city. He chose a place on the Potomac River not far from Mount Vernon, his home.

The "D.C." that is written after "Washington" stands for "District of Columbia." The District of Columbia is the tiny part of the United States that was set aside for the capital. Although the District of Columbia is between Maryland and Virginia, it is not a part of either state.

Washington is one of the most beautiful cities in the world. It is beautiful partly because it was carefully planned. It did not just grow up from a small village as many cities have. Major L'Enfant, a French engineer, was given the task of planning the city. Its streets were laid out in an interesting pattern. Many of them go out from circles like the spokes of a wheel. Fine parks and buildings help make the city beautiful, too. Many of the buildings were built by the government.

Washington became the capital of the United States in 1800, when the country was still very young. During the War of 1812 the city fell into the hands of the British and much of it was burned. But the damage was soon repaired.

The most important building in Washington is the Capitol. It is shown in the picture on this page. Here Congress meets to make the laws for the United States. On the dome of the Capitol there is a bronze statue of Freedom. Not far away from the Capitol is the White House, the home of the presidents. Nearby, too, are the Supreme Court Building and the homes of the Post Office Department, the Department of Agriculture, and many other branches of the government. The work of the national government has grown and grown, and new buildings have had to be built from time to time. The Government Printing Office in Washington is the largest printing establishment of its kind in

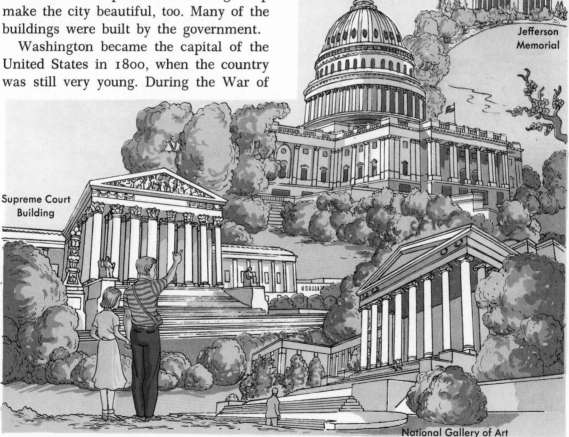

Capitol

Jefferson Memorial

Supreme Court Building

National Gallery of Art

the world. And the Library of Congress is one of the world's largest libraries.

In the city there are monuments to some famous presidents. The Washington Monument, the Lincoln Memorial, and the Jefferson Memorial are three of them.

The most famous street in Washington is Pennsylvania Avenue. Part of it runs from the Capitol to the White House. Many great parades have gone down this avenue.

The city of Washington has grown so that it fills all of the District of Columbia. One of the newer government buildings— the Pentagon—is across the Potomac in Virginia. In it are the offices of the Department of Defense. The Pentagon is one of the largest office buildings in the world. It covers 34 acres, and more than 32,000 people work in it. Many workers in Washington live in towns and cities in Maryland and Virginia. More than 1,000,000 people live in or near Washington. Many of these people work for the government.

The city has fine museums and schools. There are several universities.

A city as important and as beautiful as Washington naturally has many visitors. About two million people visit it every year. (See DISTRICT OF COLUMBIA; LINCOLN MEMORIAL; U.S. GOVERNMENT; WHITE HOUSE.)

WASHINGTON MONUMENT The monument built to honor the first president of the United States towers high above the city named for him, Washington, D.C. It is 555 feet, 5 inches tall.

The monument is shaped like an Egyptian obelisk, but it is much larger than any Egyptian obelisk. It is the tallest all-stone structure in the world. The walls are chiefly of granite but they have a facing of marble. Only the marble shows.

The structure is hollow. At the base the walls are 15 feet thick, but they are only a foot and a half thick at the top. A stairway inside leads up to an observation room 500 feet above the ground. There are 898 steps in the stairway. There is also an elevator to the observation room.

The monument was started in 1848 but was not finished until 1884. When the cornerstone was laid, a speaker said, "Build it to the skies; you cannot outreach the loftiness of his principles."

WASPS All the many kinds of wasps are close relatives of the ants and bees. Wasps can be told from their relatives by their slender waists. Like the ants and bees, they go through four stages in their lives. First they are eggs, then wormlike larvas, then pupas, and finally grown-up insects. Like many of their relatives they can sting.

Some wasps live in colonies just as honeybees do. The wasps in a colony work together. Some do one task and some another. These wasps are called social wasps. The wasps that do not live in colonies are called solitary wasps. In the pictures the paper wasp, the white-faced hornet, and the yellow jacket are social wasps.

Paper wasps and white-faced hornets build their nests of paper. They make the paper of chewed-up wood. Wasps made paper long before people did.

Each nest of a paper wasp or a white-faced hornet is the home of a whole colony. In each colony there is a queen that does all the egg laying. Most of the other wasps

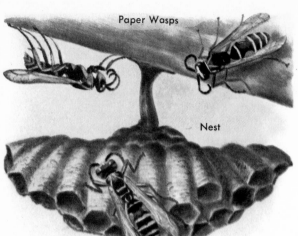

Paper Wasps

Nest

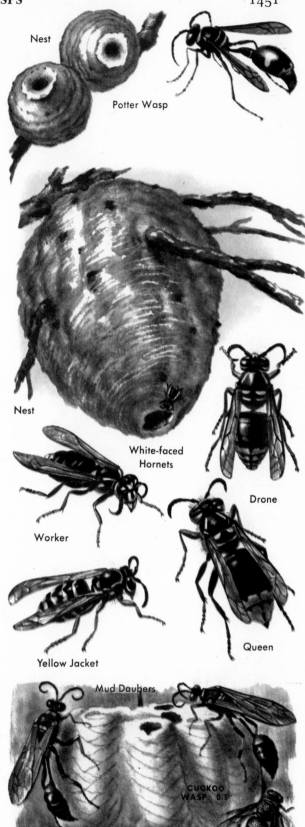

Nest

Potter Wasp

Nest

White-faced Hornets

Drone

Worker

Queen

Yellow Jacket

Mud Daubers

CUCKOO WASP 0.5

Nest

in the colony are workers. The story of every wasp colony is very much the same.

In regions with cold winters, only the queens live through the winter. In the spring each queen starts a nest of her own. As soon as a few rooms are ready she lays an egg in each one. When the eggs hatch she gathers food for the larvas. The first eggs all grow up to be workers. Then they build new cells and take care of the larvas that hatch from new eggs the queen lays. The queen does nothing for the rest of the summer but lay eggs. Late in the summer some of the young wasps that hatch are queens and males. They mate. Then all the males and workers die and the queens hide away for the winter.

The yellow jacket is another common wasp. It is a social wasp that builds big nests in the ground.

The potter wasp builds little mud jugs on twigs. Each jug is a nursery. The mother wasp lays an egg in each one and puts in some caterpillars. When a baby wasp hatches from the egg it finds the caterpillars all ready for it to eat.

The mud dauber builds mud nests of many rooms. The mother mud dauber lays one egg in each room and packs spiders in beside it for food.

The cuckoo wasp does not make a nest. It lays its eggs in a mud dauber nest while the mud dauber has gone hunting. (See ANTS; BEE.)

Over two thirds of the world is covered with water.

WATER It is wet; it can be seen easily; it can be poured. It is dry; it cannot be felt; it cannot be seen. It is hard as rock. It hardly seems possible that these three sentences are all about the same material. But they are. They are all about water.

The first sentence tells about water as it is in oceans and rivers and raindrops. It is about water when it is a liquid.

The second sentence tells about water as it is in the air around us. There it is a vapor or gas. No one can see it. But we can make it come out of hiding if we cool the air enough. Water vapor is dry. But when we cool it enough to make it change back to liquid water, it is wet again. The drops of water on the tin cup in the picture were formed from water vapor in the air.

Water is as hard as rock when freezing has changed it to a solid. Solid water, of course, is ice. Strange as it seems, ice is not wet. It is wet only when it melts.

Water may be a solid, a liquid, or a gas.

More than two thirds of the earth is covered by oceans and rivers and lakes. Besides, there is always a great deal of water in the air and in what we call dry land. Even in very dry ground there is usually a thin film of water around every particle of soil.

The oceans and lakes and rivers of the world are the homes of many living things. But even the plants and animals that live on land must have water. One reason all living things must have water is that they are made partly of water. We are, ourselves. A person can live without food far longer than he can without water.

We have to have water to drink. We need it also for keeping clean, for cooking,

Water as it boils turns into water vapor, or steam.

for making plants grow, for fighting fires, and for other things, too. One of the problems of every farm and town and city is how to get the water it needs.

Scientists have a shorthand way of writing "water"—a formula, it is called. The formula is H_2O. The H stands for hydrogen and the O for oxygen. The formula tells that water is made of hydrogen and oxygen joined together and that there are two parts of hydrogen to every one of oxygen. But no one has to know what water is made of to know that his life depends on it. (See AIR; COMPOUNDS; CONSERVATION; ELECTRICITY; EROSION; FOODS; LAKES; OCEANS; RAIN; RIVERS; SOIL; WATERFALLS; WATER SUPPLY; WATER WHEELS; WAVES.)

Herring Gull   Laughing Gull   Royal Tern

WATER BIRDS No birds can live *in* water as fish and whales and lobsters do. The birds we call water birds live on or near water and get their food from the water. There are hundreds of kinds. Many of them are excellent swimmers. Many can dive very well. Some are wonderful fliers.

The bills of many water birds are especially good for getting food from water. Some bills are built so that the water is easily strained away from the food. Some are good for skimming food from the surface of the water. Some are long and stout and are good for catching rather large fish.

The feathers of water birds are well oiled and waterproof. Many water birds have webbed feet, helpful in swimming.

Among the best-known water birds are the ducks, geese, and swans. They spend much of their time swimming about, gathering food from the surface of the water.

The loons, grebes, and penguins are expert divers as well as swimmers. They are awkward on land. The penguin uses its wings as paddles. It cannot fly at all.

Very different are the albatross and the man-of-war bird. They can fly for hours at a time over the ocean. They come down to the water only long enough to catch their food. These birds are large and have long, strong wings.

Gulls and terns are great fliers, too. The arctic tern is the champion long distance flier. Some arctic terns, in flying south in the fall and north in the spring, travel more than 20,000 miles a year.

Pelicans and cormorants spend a great deal of time perched on the shore watching for fish. A pelican has a pouch on its lower bill that makes a good food basket.

Many water birds go wading to get their food. Long legs help them in wading. Some water birds are found mostly in marshes. Some are found on seashores or the shores of lakes and ponds. Herons, cranes, spoonbills, and flamingoes are good waders.

Not all water birds are large. The stormy petrel, an ocean flier, is about as big as a swallow. The least sandpiper, a shore bird, is no bigger than a robin.

None of the water birds is a good singer. But some have loud voices. The loon is famous for its wild cry. (See BIRD MIGRATION; BIRDS; GAME BIRDS.)

Stormy Petrel

Man-of-War

Gannet

Egret

Whistling Swan   Great Auk   Booby   Great Blue Heron   Spoonbill

Puffin

Angel Falls is the highest known waterfall.

WATERFALLS On its way to a lake or a sea, a river may plunge over a steep cliff. If it does, there is a waterfall. There are more likely to be waterfalls in mountains than anywhere else.

Niagara Falls, on the border between the United States and Canada, is one of the most famous of all waterfalls. It is one of the world's wonders because such a vast amount of water pours over the cliff. But more than 70 falls are higher.

As far as anyone knows, the highest waterfall in the world is Angel Falls. It is in a wild, mountainous part of Venezuela. It was discovered by an explorer who flew over the region. Angel Falls is about 20 times as high as Niagara.

The list below shows how 20 other waterfalls compare with Niagara.

FALLS	HEIGHT	LOCATION
Angel Falls	3,212	Venezuela
Kukenaam	2,000	Venezuela
Sutherland Falls	1,904	New Zealand
Tugela	1,800	South Africa
Yosemite	1,750	California
Ribbon Falls	1,612	California
Takakkaw Falls	1,200	Canada
Trummelback	950	Switzerland
Multnomah Falls	850	Oregon
Fairy Falls	700	Washington
Bridalveil Falls	620	California
Nevada Falls	594	California
Granite Falls	350	Washington
Victoria Falls	350	South Africa
Yellowstone (lower)	308	Wyoming
Seven Falls	266	Colorado
Splendor of the Sun	225	Japan
Iguassu Falls	200	Brazil
Shoshone Falls	195	Idaho
Twin Falls	180	Idaho
Niagara Falls	167	U.S.A.—Canada

WATER PLANTS A maple tree would drown if it were covered with water. So would most of the plants we know best. They would drown because they can not get the oxygen they need from water. But there are plants that are fitted for living in water. Some live entirely under water. Some float on the surface. Some have their roots in the mud at the bottom of the water and their leaves on or above the surface. Their "feet" are under water, but their

Niagara Falls lies between Canada and the United States.

"heads" are in the air. The pictures show three common water plants.

Most of the plants that live under water in the sea are algae. We call these algae seaweeds. There are red, green, blue-green, and brown ones. Algae are simple plants. They do not have roots or leaves or flowers. But they are not all small. Some brown seaweeds are more than 100 feet long.

There are many algae in fresh water, too. Most of the fresh-water algae are green. There are many other fresh-water plants that live entirely under water. We buy some kinds for our aquariums. Eel-grass and parrot feather are two of them.

These underwater plants do not drown, because they can get oxygen from the air that is dissolved in the water. They are like fish in this way.

The plants in the pictures are only part-ly under water. The tiny duckweed, the smallest of all flowering plants, can take in air through the upper surface of its flat leaflike stem. The lotus has its roots in the mud. Its leaves take in air just as the leaves of land plants do. The cattail, too, has its roots in the mud, but it sends its leaves and flowers up high above the water. The water hyacinth is a well-known floating plant. Its leaf stalks swell out into "balloons." They are filled with air. If a leaf is broken off, it has a life preserver of its own. This plant trails its roots in the water just as duckweed does.

Although standing in water would kill most trees, a few kinds can live in shallow water. The bald cypress is one of them. When it is growing in water, this tree sends "knees" from its roots up above the water's surface. Perhaps the "knees" help the roots get oxygen from the air. No one is sure.

The mangroves are among the few flow-ering plants that can stand salt water. They grow in marshes along seacoasts in warm regions. They have prop roots that hold them up out of reach of the tides.

It is hard to believe that any plant that lives in water would have a hard time get-ting enough water. But mangroves and other flowering plants that grow in salt water look like desert plants with their small, thick-skinned leaves. The salt hin-ders the water from entering the roots. Some plants living in bogs have a hard time getting enough water, too. They do not have many roots. Perhaps their roots are harmed by poisons in the water. Some bog plants are able to get along with so little water that they can also grow on dry, rocky cliffs. (See ALGAE; XEROPHYTES.)

Cattails

Duckweed

American Lotus

WATER SUPPLY A billion gallons a day! This is the amount of water it takes for some of the world's biggest cities. The people of even the biggest city do not drink that much water in a day. They use a great deal of water for drinking, but they use much more in other ways.

In homes water is used for bathing, washing clothes, cleaning the house, and cooking. It is used to carry waste down into sewers and away. It may be used to carry heat from a furnace to all the rooms of the house. Home owners use water, too, for watering lawns and gardens.

A city uses water for fighting fire and for keeping its streets clean. It also uses water to keep the grass and trees of its parks green and growing and to fill pools for swimming and bathing. Some cities also use water to turn giant generators to make electric power.

But in a big city the greatest part of the water is used in factories. Many kinds of things cannot be manufactured without the use of an enormous amount of water.

Some cities are very fortunate. They have a huge supply of water right at their front door. Chicago is one of these lucky cities. It is on the shores of Lake Michigan. St. Louis has the great Mississippi River flowing past. Many of the world's big cities are on lakes or big rivers that furnish them with water. But some cities must bring water from many miles away. New York and Los Angeles are two cities that have had to build great aqueducts in order to bring water from far away. Both these big cities are near the ocean. But ocean water has too much salt in it to be used. The water in a city's water supply must be fresh water.

Some cities get their water from artificial lakes. These lakes are formed by the building of dams across streams. Some cities get their water from wells. The wells gather in water from layers of sand and rock underground. In small towns and on farms many people have their own wells.

Even cities and towns that have plenty of water may not have a good water supply. For the water may not be fit to use. There are impurities of many kinds in water.

The most dangerous of the impurities found in water are disease germs. Typhoid fever is one of the diseases carried by water. Even water that is sparkling clear and good-tasting may have disease germs in it. Disease germs are far too small to be seen without a microscope.

Mud is another common impurity. Mud spoils the taste of water. Besides, muddy water is not fit for laundry work or bathing or manufacturing.

Some water has so much mineral material dissolved in it that it is called hard water. Hard water is, as a rule, pleasant to drink. But if it is used in cleaning and laundering, it uses up a great deal of soap. Most factory owners do not want hard water for their manufacturing.

Water is not only stored in lakes but also in snow and ice. It takes ten inches of snow to melt into one inch of water.

Underground water is obtained by means of springs and wells.

Aqueducts make it possible to carry water for long distances and to places where water is scarce.

Water may have impurities in it that give it a bad odor or color as well as a bad taste. Some water, for instance, has a gas called "rotten-egg gas" dissolved in it. And some water contains so much iron that it stains clothes washed in it.

It is next to impossible for a big city to get enough water that is safe and satisfactory without being purified. Almost all cities purify their water in some way.

Adding chlorine is a very common way of purifying water. It kills disease germs. It is a poison, but not enough is used to hurt the people who drink the water.

If cities must use muddy water, they usually filter it. They make it sink through beds of sand that strain out the mud and many of the disease germs.

Some cities add chemicals to their water to keep it from being too hard. Some shoot their water up into the air so that sunshine and air can help purify it. Some combine two or three ways of purifying water.

In small towns and on farms families may have to purify their own water. Boil-

ing water kills the germs in it. Small home filters can be used to take out mud.

A city also has to see to it that water gets to where it is needed. Almost every city has a pumping station as a part of its water supply system. In a few cases water comes down to a city from lakes or streams high in the mountains and does not have to be pumped to where it is used. Under every city there is a great network of pipes to carry water. They are called water mains.

The problem of getting a good supply of water is nothing new. Three thousand years ago the city of Tyre had a hard time getting the water it needed. Tyre was on an island in the Mediterranean Sea. Not only was the water in the sea salty but the water in the wells dug on the island was salty, too. The people of Tyre dug wells far back from shore on the mainland near by. Then they built a stone-lined ditch, or aqueduct, to carry the water down to the shore. There it was loaded on boats and taken to the island. A thousand years later Rome had great aqueducts that brought water from springs as far away as 50 miles. Ruins of the aqueducts still stand. (See AQUEDUCT; HYDRAULICS.)

WATER WHEELS Thousands of years ago men learned how to harness the water of rivers and waterfalls. They made it turn water wheels. Then they used the water wheels to turn other machines.

The pictures show two old-fashioned kinds of water wheels. One has paddles around the edge. The other has buckets. The one with paddles is called an undershot water wheel. The water runs under it. It strikes the paddles and turns the wheel. The one with buckets is an overshot water wheel. The water travels to the top of the wheel through a trough or pipe of some kind and falls into one bucket after another. The water that fills the buckets is heavy enough to make the wheel turn. As soon as a bucket reaches the bottom of the wheel, the water in it spills out. In many of the early mills in the United States the big grinding stones were turned by water wheels like these.

Most water wheels of today are turbines. A turbine is a water wheel or a group of several water wheels shut up inside a case. Each wheel has many blades. Water flows into the turbine, hits the blades, and makes the wheel or wheels turn.

The most important use of turbines is in electric power plants. There are many big power plants beside rivers or waterfalls. The water of the river or falls turns water turbines. The turbines turn great electric generators. Power plants in which the generators are turned by water turbines are called hydroelectric plants. "Hydroelectric" means "water electric." (See ELECTRICITY; FACTORIES.)

WAVES Wind pushes up waves on seas and lakes and ponds. Everyone who has seen an ocean or a sea or a lake or a pond has seen waves. They are so common that long ago, before there was an alphabet of letters, people used to draw a wavy line to stand for water.

Sometimes waves are just little ripples. But the wind may push up waves that are

Undershot Wheel

Water from below pushes the paddles.

Water from the stream drops into the buckets of the wheel and makes it turn.

Overshot Wheel

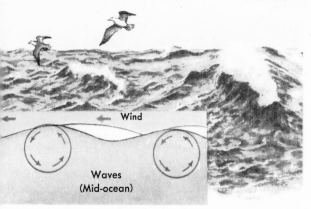

Wind

Waves
(Mid-ocean)

as tall as a house. They may even be as tall as a five-story building.

Waves far out from shore usually have smooth tops, or crests. But big waves near shore often break into white foam at the top. Waves that do are called breakers. The lines of foam are "whitecaps."

Big waves can wear away the shores of lakes and seas. They pick up sand and gravel and use them as tools. Even if a shore is made up of solid rock, waves can wear it away. Sometimes they make big caves at the edge of the water.

Waves do not always wear away the shores they wash against. They may build up the shores instead. They may make a very broad, sandy beach.

Not all waves are caused by wind. The biggest waves are caused by earthquakes or volcanic eruptions under the sea. Such giant waves are called tidal waves. Some of them are so big that they wash away whole villages. The tidal wave after the famous eruption of Krakatao in the East Indies in 1883 killed 35,000 people. (See EARTHQUAKES; LAKES; OCEANS; TIDES; VOLCANOES.)

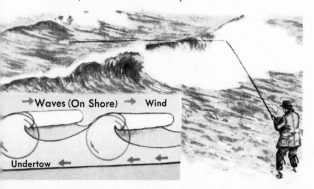

Waves (On Shore) → Wind

Undertow ←

WEAPONS Many animals have weapons that are a part of their bodies. The sharp teeth and claws of the tiger, the horns of a buffalo, the poison fangs of a rattlesnake, and the sting of a bee are good examples. People do not have any such weapons as these. But thousands of years ago our ancestors learned how to make weapons.

Stones, clubs, and stone-tipped spears were among the weapons of the cave men. The story of weapons from cave-man days till today is a very long one. The pictures show a few of the steps in it.

Bows and arrows, lances, javelins, pikes, sabers, scimitars, battle-axes, and crossbows were used in ancient and medieval times. Such weapons gave way to guns when gunpowder came into use in warfare

Early man used a club as a weapon.

about four centuries ago. Guns of many sizes and kinds have been invented. Some have had such strange names as blunderbuss and bazooka.

In time explosives much more powerful than gunpowder were invented. They were used in bombs, rockets, mines, hand grenades, and torpedoes.

War was greatly speeded up when horses and sailing vessels gave way to engine-driven trucks, tanks, and battleships. It changed still more when airplanes carried the fighting into the air and submarines carried it below the surface of the sea.

The discovery of new ways of getting energy from atoms was another important step in the story of weapons. Atomic bombs —"A-bombs"—helped bring about an end to World War II. Hydrogen bombs, developed since World War II, are even more destructive than A-bombs. Cannons that fire atomic shells and other atomic weapons are now being made.

All early weapons were meant for close fighting. The fighters were on foot, on horseback, in chariots drawn by horses, or in boats that came close to one another. Now much fighting is done against troops or targets too far away to be seen—in some cases hundreds of miles away. Many modern weapons are long-range weapons.

It is said that the warfare of the future will be mostly "push-button warfare." Pilotless bombers and rockets will be guided to their targets from the ground. The guiding will be done by radar or something similar. Such weapons are called "guided missiles." The V-rockets used by Germany during World War II were guided missiles. They showed what powerful weapons guided missiles can be.

Any cave man could swing a club or hurl a spear at an enemy. Today's weapons are much more complicated. A soldier must have a great deal of training to be able to use some of them. Such training is expensive. And the weapons themselves are much, much more expensive than the weapons of long ago. Countries pay out enormous sums for weapons. They spend a great deal of money, too, in working out ideas for newer weapons.

TYPES OF WEAPONS

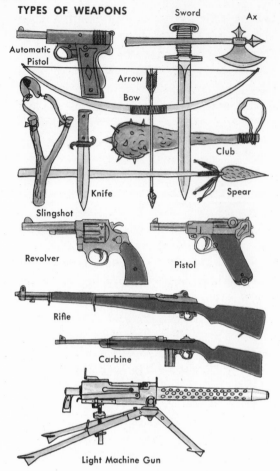

Automatic Pistol · Sword · Ax · Arrow · Bow · Club · Knife · Spear · Slingshot · Revolver · Pistol · Rifle · Carbine · Light Machine Gun

Very few people know about the very newest weapons a country has. Countries keep their new weapons as much of a secret as they can. Until nations work out some way of living together peacefully, the race to get newer weapons will go on. (See AIRPLANES; ARMOR; ARMY; ATOMS; EXPLOSIVES; NAVY; ROCKETS; SHIPS; SUBMARINES; U.S. ARMED FORCES.)

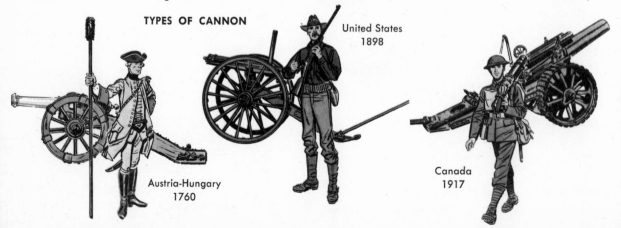

TYPES OF CANNON

Austria-Hungary 1760

United States 1898

Canada 1917

WEATHER What is the weather going to be? This question is really several questions in one. It means: Will the sky be cloudy or clear? Will any rain or snow fall? How warm or cool will it be? How much moisture will there be in the air? From what direction will the wind come? Will the wind be gentle or strong?

Rain, snow, hail, sleet, frost, and dew are all a part of the weather. So are cold waves, heat waves, clouds, breezes, gales, thunderstorms, and hurricanes.

In some parts of the world the weather stays very much the same day after day. In other places it changes often. A summer day that starts out to be bright and sunshiny may end with a thunderstorm. In the same way a cold and cloudy winter morning may be followed by a clear and springlike afternoon.

In places where the weather changes often, everyone is interested in it. But not everyone wants the same kind of weather. A farmer may want a rainy day because his corn needs rain. His neighbor may want a sunshiny day because it is time for him to harvest his hay. Some people may be glad to see a heavy snowstorm because they want to go skiing. Others may not like the snow at all because it blocks the roads and makes traveling hard. Not everyone is happy when there is a week of warm, sunshiny weather in early spring. Some people know that the snow is melting so fast that rivers will flood.

Even if a person does not mind heat or cold or rain or snow, the weather is important to him. Bad weather may ruin crops so that food will cost more. It may cause forest fires, kill stock on the ranges, flood homes, and slow up the mail. The weather affects the lives of all of us in a great many ways.

Often in the summer we hear people say, "It's not the heat; it's the humidity." This saying is quite often true. "Humidity" means the amount of moisture in the air. When there is a great deal of moisture in

Summer showers often take people by surprise.

the air, a hot day seems much hotter than if the air were drier. Our bodies have a way of keeping themselves cool. They perspire, and the perspiration evaporates. When it evaporates, it cools us off. If there is a great deal of moisture in the air, perspiration cannot evaporate fast. It cannot cool us off very well.

Another common saying is one of Mark Twain's: "Everyone talks about the weather, but no one ever does anything about it." Today this saying is not altogether true.

We have learned to make the weather inside our houses anything we want it to be. We can make the air warmer. Or we can cool it off. We can put more moisture in it if it is too dry. Or, if it is too damp, we can take some of the moisture out of it. We can turn on lights if it is dark and cloudy out of doors. And by simply turning the

Modern rainmakers drop dry ice on the clouds.

Clouds are important weather guides.

A tornado is a violent, whirling wind with a funnel-shaped cloud.

Clouds help break the sunlight into rays.

Thunderstorms over land occur mostly in the summer.

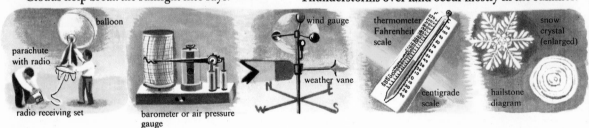

switch of an electric fan we can start a pleasant breeze blowing.

Even out of doors we have begun to experiment with changing the weather. We have made fogs disappear from airplane landing fields—and a few times we have caused rain by dropping dry ice on clouds from airplanes. But probably we will usu-ally have to take the weather as it comes. Even if we could change the weather easily, there would be many quarrels about what it should be. (See AIR CONDITIONING; CLIMATE; CLOUDBURST; CLOUDS; DEW; FLOODS; FOG; FROST; HAIL; LIGHTNING; RAIN; SNOW; STORMS; U.S. WEATHER BUREAU; WIND.)

WEBSTER, DANIEL (1782-1852) Born when the United States was a very new nation, Daniel Webster became one of its greatest orators. He was also one of its most noted statesmen.

As a boy Daniel lived with his parents in a small town in New Hampshire. His family was a hard-working pioneer family, but Daniel was too frail to do hard work. He was also so shy that he would never speak a piece in school. No one in his school, however, could learn his lessons more quickly or more easily.

The boy made such wonderful progress with his studies that his family decided that he must go to college. It meant hardships for the rest of the family, but they were willing to put up with them.

Daniel went to Dartmouth College, not far from his home in New Hampshire. He studied law. But after he graduated from college he taught in an academy for a time so that he could send his brother Ezekiel to college. He knew that a paying law practice cannot be built up quickly. He began practicing law, however, when he was still only 23. He started his law practice in Boston, but when his father became ill he went home. Soon after his father's death he set up a law office in Portsmouth, N.H.

Soon Webster became known as a fine orator. It is not surprising that the people of New Hampshire chose him to be one of their representatives in Congress. Later he moved to Massachusetts and in 1823 was elected to Congress from that state. From then on almost until his death he served his country either as a member of Congress or as a member of the president's cabinet. Under three presidents he was secretary of state.

One of Webster's most famous speeches was made at the laying of the cornerstone of the Bunker Hill monument in Boston. Another was made on the 200th anniversary of the landing of the Pilgrims. A third was made at the deaths of Thomas Jefferson and John Adams. These two ex-presidents died on the same day—July 4, 1826.

Webster, during his career in Washington, did everything he could to build the states into a strong nation. He knew that the nation could never be strong if any or all of the states put themselves first and the nation second. He made this motto famous: "Liberty and Union, now and forever, one and inseparable!" (See BUNKER HILL; UNITED STATES HISTORY.)

Daniel Webster, a forceful orator, always drew crowds of listeners.

Webster wrote the first great American dictionary.

WEBSTER, NOAH (1758-1843) How do you spell this word? How is this word pronounced? What does this word mean? People, when they are still very young, learn where to find answers to such questions. They learn to look in a dictionary. And in a great many cases they look in a Webster's dictionary.

Noah Webster was born in Connecticut while Connecticut was still a colony—before there was a United States of America. He could trace his ancestry back on both his mother's side and his father's side to colonial governors: Governor William Bradford of Plymouth, and Governor John Webster of Connecticut.

As a young man he went to college at Yale, but he left college for a while to fight in the Revolutionary War. He then went back to Yale to finish his college work.

After Webster left college he taught school for a while and then practiced law. He was elected to a number of public offices, and he wrote many pamphlets. But he is famous for two books—a spelling book and his dictionary. When he was teaching school, he saw that these two books were needed.

The spelling book was the first part of the *Grammatical Institute of the English Language*. The second part was a grammar and the third a reader. The first part —the spelling book—was published in 1783. It soon came to be called simply *Webster's Spelling Book* or *Blue-Backed Speller*. It sold for over 100 years. More than 60,000,000 copies were printed.

It took Webster 20 years to write his dictionary. Part of this time he spent visiting scholars in England and France.

The first edition of the dictionary was published in 1828 and the second in 1840. The first edition contained 12,000 words and between 30,000 and 40,000 definitions that had never been in a dictionary before. With his dictionary Webster did a great deal to make spelling simpler. For instance, he changed the spelling of "colour" to "color," "centre" to "center," and "waggon". to "wagon."

Webster's dictionary is still being printed by the millions. Of course, changes in it have been made since Webster's time. Words that Webster never heard or even dreamed of have been added. A *Webster's New International Dictionary* of today has more than 600,000 words. This dictionary is so well known that many an argument about words is settled by "What does Webster say?" (See ENGLISH LANGUAGE.)

WEEDS Any plant that is growing where we do not want it to grow may be considered a weed. Corn in a rose garden is a weed. So is a rosebush growing in a cornfield. Even an elm tree growing among pine trees is a weed if only pine trees are wanted in the forest. Of course, corn in a cornfield, roses in a rose garden, and elm trees in our yards are not weeds.

Some kinds of plants are weeds no matter where they are growing. Cockleburs, quack grass, and ragweed, for example, are always weeds. No one ever wants them.

Weeds are not wanted for several reasons. They hurt gardens and fields and lawns in several different ways.

Weeds take water and minerals from the soil. They may take so much that the wanted plants do not get all they need.

Many weeds grow tall. They shut off sunlight from the plants we want. Without sunlight green plants cannot grow.

Weeds may grow so thick that the plants we are trying to raise are too crowded to grow well. Those we want may be actually smothered by weeds.

Some weeds are vines. They may climb up on useful plants and pull them down. Dodder, which is a vine, does even more harm. It "steals" all its food from the plant on which it is growing.

The plants we raise have many insect enemies. In a weedy field or garden there are many hiding places for insects.

Some weeds are poisonous. They may make animals sick that eat them.

Weeds spoil the looks of lawns and gardens, too. Even if they did no harm, we would try to get rid of them.

No one ever means to plant weeds. But some weeds, like foxtail and mustard, have such tiny seeds that they can easily get mixed in with garden seeds and grain. Most weeds plant themselves. Their seeds have different ways of traveling. Some go by air. Some go by water. Some are carried by animals. Tumbleweeds dry up and roll away, scattering seeds as they go.

Many weeds are annuals—that is, they grow from seed in the spring, form seeds of their own, and die in the fall. Other weeds start growing one year, live through the winter, and die at the end of their second summer. These weeds are called biennials. Some weeds live on year after year. They are called perennials. It helps in fighting weeds to know whether they are annuals, biennials, or perennials. If they are annuals, it is important to keep them from going to seed. If they are biennials or perennials, it is important to kill the roots.

Hoeing and plowing get rid of many weeds. Of course, weeds can be pulled up by hand in a small garden or in a lawn. Chemicals are a help in killing some weeds. On a lawn a chemical weed-killer can be used that will kill the weeds without hurting the grass. Some birds are our helpers in fighting weeds. They eat weed seeds.

Some of the weeds in the United States came from other lands. The Russian thistle is one. Galinsoga, a little weed very common in gardens, is another.

One good thing can be said for weeds. They sometimes hold soil in place and keep it from washing away after heavy rains. This help is especially important in areas where there are already many gullies. (See BIRDS; SEEDS; SOIL; WILD FLOWERS.)

Sticktight

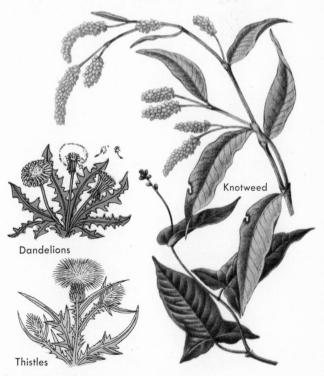

Dandelions

Thistles

Knotweed

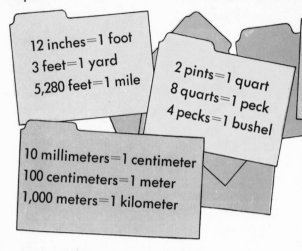

12 inches = 1 foot
3 feet = 1 yard
5,280 feet = 1 mile

2 pints = 1 quart
8 quarts = 1 peck
4 pecks = 1 bushel

16 fluid ounces = 1 pint
2 pints = 1 quart
4 quarts = 1 gallon

16 drams = 1 ounce
16 ounces = 1 pound
2,000 pounds = 1 ton

10 millimeters = 1 centimeter
100 centimeters = 1 meter
1,000 meters = 1 kilometer

WEIGHTS AND MEASURES Gallons, tons, bushels, acres, yards—such measures as these are very important in our lives. Measuring is a part of almost all our trading and of almost all our manufacturing and of almost all our building. How could we buy and sell such things as oil, coal, grain, land, and cloth if we had no measures? How could we build skyscrapers and bridges or manufacture jet planes and automobiles without them? Scientists, moreover, depend on measures to help them make discoveries. If for some reason we had to give up all our ways of weighing and measuring, we would have to go back to extremely simple ways of living.

People would have to live very simply indeed to get along without measuring length. In the United States length is measured chiefly in inches, feet, yards, and miles. These, we say, are units of length. Our early ancestors measured length long before there were any such units. When a cave man, for instance, wished to make a new spear just the length of his old one he could measure the new one by the old one.

But soon the people of long ago found that they needed some kind of measuring rod for measuring many different things. In order to get such a measuring rod, they turned to their own bodies.

No one knows exactly when men began using body measures, but we do know that in ancient times four body measures were much used. One was the cubit. This was the distance from the point of the elbow to the end of the middle finger. The second was the span. A span was the distance from the end of the thumb to the end of the little finger when the hand was spread out. The third was the palm. This was the breadth of the four fingers held together. The fourth body measure was the digit. The digit was the breadth of the first finger or the middle finger.

Our early ancestors needed other ways of measuring length, too. A cave man might want to tell how far away a herd of mammoths was. He could not tell the distance in arm lengths. One of the earliest ways of answering "How far away is it?" was to tell how long it would take to go there. This way of measuring distances was common among the Indians until recent times. Saying that some place was three suns away meant that to get there it would take three days. Even now we say that a house is only a ten-minute walk from a railroad station or perhaps a half-hour's drive from a shopping center.

Counting steps was another way of measuring distance in early times. We still often "step off" distances.

To the early Babylonians, Egyptians, and Hebrews the cubit was the most important measure of length. But it was no longer the crude measure it had been in the beginning. In the beginning every person had a cubit all his own—the length of his own forearm. But with the beginning of trade, it was important that everyone who was trading use the same cubit. Governments then stepped in and decided how long the cubit would be. In some cases the governments may have used the forearm of the ruler. At least we know that the governments changed their minds from time to time about how long the cubit should be.

Some very old measuring rods have been found in ancient ruins. In the ruins of the famous temple of Karnak, in Egypt, for example, a two-cubit ruler was found.

Just when the foot, which gets its name from the human foot, became a standard measure no one is sure. We do know that the Greeks used it. The Romans borrowed it from the Greeks and made it the chief measure of length for short distances all through the great Roman Empire. The inch in the beginning was the breadth of the thumb. The Romans divided a foot into 12 inches just as we do today, but their foot and their inches were not just the same length as ours.

The mile came down to us from the Romans, too. "Mile" is short for *mille passuum,* the Latin words for "a thousand paces." The Roman pace was a double step and was five feet long.

Such a measure as the foot cannot be expected to stay the same unless somewhere there is an actual measuring rod, carefully cared for, which shows exactly how long it should be. The Romans had such rods. They kept them in a temple. But they were lost at the fall of the Roman Empire. During the Middle Ages almost every town and city of Europe had its own measuring rods. It took a long time to work out standards suitable to whole countries.

There are many stories of how standard measures were decided on. King David of Scotland decided back in the 12th century that an inch was to be the average width of "the thowmys (thumbs) of iij (three) men, that is to say an mekill man and a man of messurabil statur and of a lytell man. The thoums (thumbs) are to be messurit at the rut of the nayll." It is easy to see that spelling as well as measures have changed since his time. The English king Henry I is said to have started with

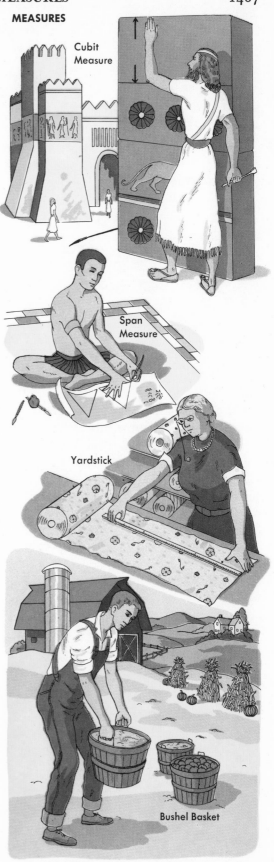

MEASURES

Cubit Measure

Span Measure

Yardstick

Bushel Basket

the yard in working out measures for England. He decided that a yard was to be the distance from the tip of his nose to the end of his thumb. At another time the English parliament decided that an inch was to be the length of three good grains of barley laid end to end.

In the days of the American colonies almost every colony had a different yard. Of course, if the yard differed, the foot and the inch and the mile also differed. After the United States became a nation a metal yardstick was made as a standard measure for the whole country. The metal yardstick was kept in Washington.

About 150 years ago the people of France decided to throw out all their old measures and make an entirely new system. They would use as their chief measure of length the meter, and this would be one ten-millionth of the distance from the equator to the North Pole. Whether they found exactly one ten-millionth of the distance from the equator to the Pole is not certain. But they did make the meter a very important measure. Their whole system of weighing and measuring gets its name from the meter. It is called the metric system. Scientists all over the world now use the metric system in much of their work.

The standard measuring rod for the United States is now a meter measure made mostly of platinum. The standard yard is $\frac{3600}{3937}$ of this meter. The measure is protected very carefully. It is always kept at the same temperature because metals expand with heat and contract when cooled.

Other units of measure had as long and complicated a history as the units of length. We now measure land in acres and square miles. One early way of measuring land was to tell the amount of seed it would take to plant it. Another was to tell how long it would take to plow it. Still another was to tell how many oxen or plows it would take to keep it cultivated.

Of course, before men could measure land by the seed it would take to plant it,

they had to be able to measure the seed. At different times materials were measured by the handful, the hornful, and the gourdful. No one knows the story of the bushel and the gallon, our most important units of dry and liquid measure. We do know that quart is short for "quarter-gallon."

Exactly how long ago people needed measures of weight no one is sure. Probably no great need was felt until trade in such metals as gold and silver began.

When early people looked about them for something they could use as weights, they saw that one grain of barley or wheat is very much like another. These grains were very common as early weights. We still use the grain as a unit of weight in weighing gold and silver and drugs even though we no longer use actual grains of wheat and barley as weights. The seed of the carob, a Mediterranean evergreen, was used as a weight in eastern countries. Diamonds are still weighed in carats, a unit that can be traced back to carob seeds.

For weighing bulky things grains were of no use. The name of one unit in the English table of weights suggests a way in which early peoples measured bulky things. This unit is the stone.

"Pound" comes from a Latin word meaning "the weight." The pound became a very important measure during Roman times. The Romans spread its use over the whole Roman Empire just as they did that of the foot and the mile.

Modern measures are very accurate partly because scientists need accurate measures for their experiments. Today scientists can measure in millionths of inches.

For years there has been talk in America of putting aside pounds, yards, miles, bushels, and gallons and using metric measures instead. The metric tables are certainly much easier to learn. Perhaps in time Americans will see such signs as "Cider—15c a liter"; "Sugar—15c a kilogram"; and "St. Louis — 50 kilometers away." (See SCALES AND WEIGHING.)

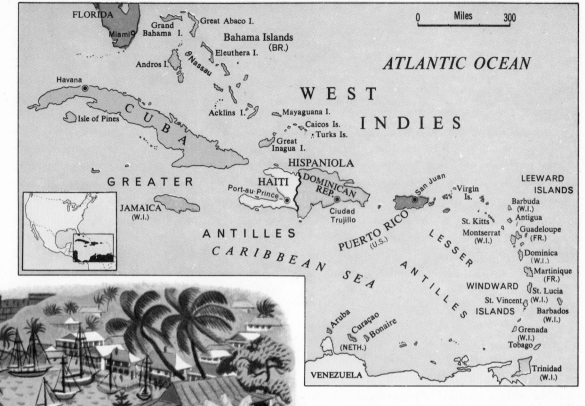

The colorful towns and port cities attract tourists.

WEST INDIES A long string of islands stretches in a curve from Florida to South America. They separate the Caribbean Sea from the Atlantic Ocean. These islands are called the West Indies.

Columbus discovered many of the West Indies on his trips to the New World. His first landing was on a small island in the group. Probably the islands got their name because Columbus had hoped to find an easy way to India and the Indies near by— the islands we now call the East Indies.

The West Indies are made up of three groups of islands: the Bahamas, the Greater Antilles, and the Lesser Antilles. The four largest islands of the West Indies— Cuba, Hispaniola, Jamaica, and Puerto Rico—are all in the Greater Antilles.

The people of Cuba rule themselves. So do the people of Haiti and of the Domini-

can Republic — the two countries into which Hispaniola is divided. Puerto Rico and some of the Virgin Islands are outlying parts of the United States. In 1958, Jamaica, Trinidad-Tobago, Barbados, St. Kitts, and several other islands formed a federation called The West Indies. Someday this group of islands may become a dominion of the British Commonwealth of Nations.

These tropical islands make good vacation spots when northern United States is covered with ice and snow. But they are much more than pleasure spots. They are known as the "sugar islands." Thousands of tons of sugar are shipped from the islands each year. Mostly in early fall, hurricanes often do great damage to the crops and to the homes and beautiful resorts.

On the islands some people live. in very simple ways. Others live in beautiful homes on wide city avenues. In some places it is easy for a visitor from the United States to imagine that he is in another part of the world altogether.

WEST VIRGINIA On a map this small mountainous state looks like an oval pan with two handles. It is hard to decide whether West Virginia should be called a Northeastern state or a South Atlantic state. It is between the North and the South. It is between the East and the Midwest, too. It does not touch the Atlantic.

Not until 1863 did West Virginia become a state. But it was not new country. It had been part of the Virginia Colony and then of the state of Virginia. George Washington surveyed lands there for Lord Fairfax in 1747 and 1748. He built forts for protection against Indians. Despite troubles with Indians, settlers came into this western part of Virginia. After the Revolutionary War the number of settlements grew. West-flowing streams were used to ship farm products, coal, and lumber to markets. The people looked to the Ohio and the west more than to the Atlantic.

The sturdy farmers and businessmen of western Virginia held with the North on the slavery question. When Virginia withdrew from the Union in 1861, western Virginia rebelled against Virginia. The people made plans for a new state. Many of them did not want the new state to have Virginia in its name. At first, it was to be called "Kanawha" after the chief river. Later, after a hot debate, "West Virginia" won.

Today West Virginia means "The Coal Bin of the World" to some people. They have driven through the coal mining valleys where there are whole strings of towns much alike. Railroad tracks, trains of coal cars, and the highways seem to fill the valleys. In each town a tall wooden coal tipple rises high above the other buildings. From the tipple a long, covered chute leads halfway up the steep slope to the mine opening. Loaded mine cars carry coal inside the chute from the mine to the tipple. In the tipple the coal is cleaned, sorted, made ready for shipping away.

In many coal mining towns the houses are lined along a single street. Some houses seem to hang from hillsides. Crowded in are a few stores and a schoolhouse. Bituminous coal by the thousands of tons is shipped from these coal-mining towns. West Virginia mines more of this coal than any other state.

To some people, West Virginia means factories. Wheeling and Weirton are steel centers. The Ohio and Kanawha valleys are among the fastest-growing chemical manufacturing districts in the country. Coal, petroleum, gas, salt, water, and air are used to make plastics, nylon, and many other new materials. At Chester and Newell there are modern pottery plants.

State Flower: Rhododendron

State Flag

State Seal

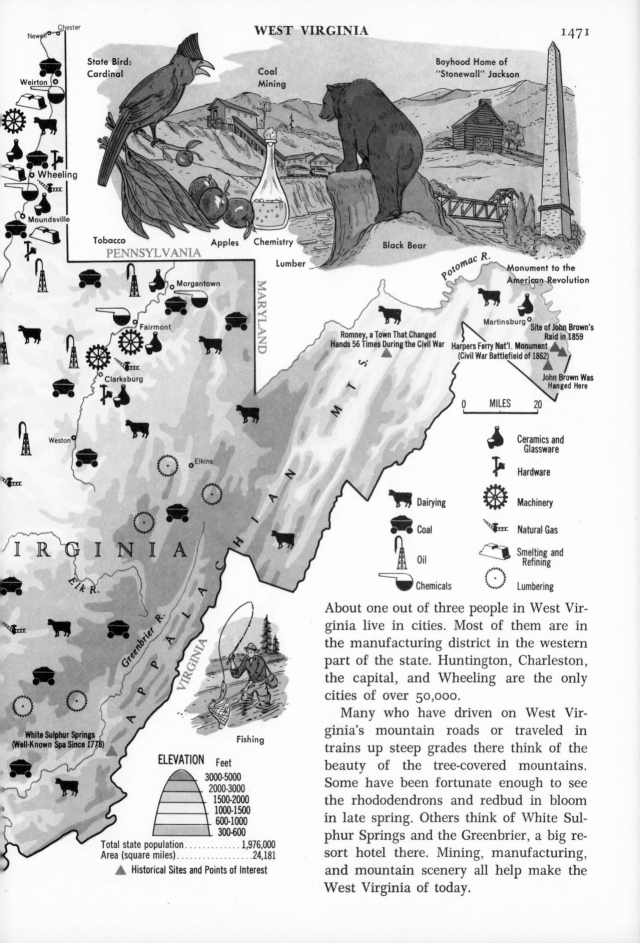

WEST VIRGINIA

1471

State Bird: Cardinal

Coal Mining

Boyhood Home of "Stonewall" Jackson

Tobacco

Apples   Chemistry

Lumber

Black Bear

PENNSYLVANIA

MARYLAND

Chester
Newell
Weirton
Wheeling
Moundsville

Morgantown

Fairmont

Clarksburg

Weston

Elkins

V I R G I N I A

Elk R.

Greenbrier R.

A P P A L A C H I A N   M T S.

VIRGINIA

Potomac R.

Monument to the American Revolution

Martinsburg

Romney, a Town That Changed Hands 56 Times During the Civil War

Site of John Brown's Raid in 1859

Harpers Ferry Nat'l. Monument (Civil War Battlefield of 1862)

John Brown Was Hanged Here

0   MILES   20

Ceramics and Glassware

Hardware

Machinery

Dairying

Coal

Oil

Chemicals

Natural Gas

Smelting and Refining

Lumbering

Fishing

White Sulphur Springs (Well-Known Spa Since 1778)

ELEVATION Feet

3000-5000
2000-3000
1500-2000
1000-1500
600-1000
300-600

Total state population............. 1,976,000
Area (square miles).................24,181
▲ Historical Sites and Points of Interest

About one out of three people in West Virginia live in cities. Most of them are in the manufacturing district in the western part of the state. Huntington, Charleston, the capital, and Wheeling are the only cities of over 50,000.

Many who have driven on West Virginia's mountain roads or traveled in trains up steep grades there think of the beauty of the tree-covered mountains. Some have been fortunate enough to see the rhododendrons and redbud in bloom in late spring. Others think of White Sulphur Springs and the Greenbrier, a big resort hotel there. Mining, manufacturing, and mountain scenery all help make the West Virginia of today.

FAMILY TREE OF WHALES

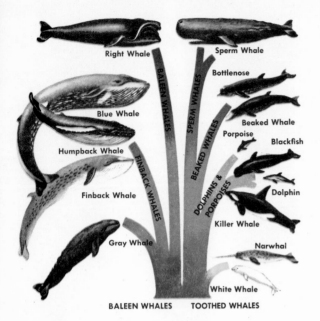

Right Whale

Sperm Whale

Bottlenose

Blue Whale

Beaked Whale

Porpoise

Blackfish

Humpback Whale

BALEEN WHALES

SPERM WHALES

BEAKED WHALES

DOLPHINS & PORPOISES

FINBACK WHALES

Finback Whale

Dolphin

Killer Whale

Gray Whale

Narwhal

White Whale

BALEEN WHALES   TOOTHED WHALES

WHALES The blue whale is the biggest animal that ever lived. It is even bigger than any of the giant dinosaurs of long ago. As the family tree shows, there are more than a dozen kinds of whales. Not all whales are enormous. Some dolphins and porpoises are only a few feet long.

All whales live in water, most of them in the sea. Many people think that whales are fish, but they are not. They are mammals.

Four things show that whales are mammals instead of fish. Whales breathe with lungs, not gills. They are warm-blooded. They have hair, even though it consists of only a few bristles. And whale babies get milk from their mothers.

A baby whale is called a calf. A blue whale calf is much bigger than an elephant.

Whales are often found in very cold water. Under its skin a whale has a very thick layer of fat that protects it from the cold. This layer is called blubber.

A whale must come to the top of the water to get air. It has to blow out the stale air from its lungs before it can breathe in fresh air. When it blows out the stale air, we say that the whale is spouting.

The blue whale lives on very tiny plants and animals. It has no teeth. Instead, it has plates of whalebone, or baleen, in its mouth. These plates have bristles at the edges that act as strainers. As the family

INTERNATIONAL WHALING REGULATIONS

A modern whaler is a factory ship.

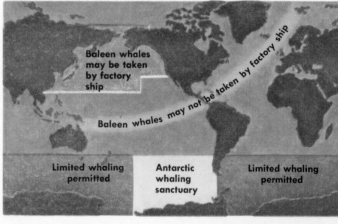

Baleen whales may be taken by factory ship

Baleen whales may not be taken by factory ship

Limited whaling permitted

Antarctic whaling sanctuary

Limited whaling permitted

Combines harvest, thresh, and clean the wheat.

tree shows, there are other whalebone whales. But some whales have strong teeth and eat large sea creatures. The killer whale is one of the meat-eating whales. It is sometimes called the "wolf of the sea."

Whale oil and whalebone are useful. For many, many years whaling vessels have gone in search of whales. The big whaling vessels of today are floating factories. To keep the whales from being killed off, nations have joined together to make rules about whaling. (See AMBERGRIS; ESKIMOS; MAMMALS.)

WHEAT No one knows what plant our early ancestors first learned to raise. Perhaps it was wheat. At least wheat has been raised for many thousands of years. The ancient Egyptians raised it. So did the Babylonians. And it was one of the five sacred grains the ancient Chinese planted in honor of their gods. Today it is one of our most important food plants.

Size Comparison of Blue Whale, Elephant, and Man

Wheat belongs to the grass family. It is therefore a cousin of corn, oats, rye, rice, and barley.

This grain can be raised in a great many parts of the world. There are different kinds to fit different climates. Some kinds of wheat need more water than others. Some kinds can stand more heat or more cold than others. Some grow faster than others. Scientists are always working with wheat, trying to develop kinds that will be sturdier and will yield more grain.

Some of the wheat raised in America is spring wheat, and some is winter wheat. Spring wheat is planted in the spring. It is harvested in late summer. Winter wheat is planted in the fall. Blankets of snow protect the young plants during the winter. The wheat is ready to be harvested the following spring or summer.

Grains of wheat are wheat seeds. Much of the wheat we raise is made into flour. From the flour we make bread, cake, cookies, crackers, puddings, macaroni, and spaghetti. Of course, there are other kinds of flour made from other grains. But in the United States much more wheat flour is used than any other kind. Americans use over 20 billion pounds a year. Our meals would be different if we had no wheat. (See FLOUR; GRASSES; SEEDS.)

WHEELS Try to imagine a world without wheels. There would be no trains, no automobiles, no airplanes, no wagons, and no bicycles. There would be no toys with wheels, no clocks or watches, and none of many kinds of factory machines. Our whole way of living would have to be changed if all wheels disappeared.

The wheel is surely one of the most important inventions ever made. But no one knows who made it. It probably was invented somewhere in Mesopotamia, the Land of the Two Rivers. At least we know that the wheel was in use several thousand years ago in that land.

The ancestor of the wheel was probably a log. Men discovered that they could use logs as rollers in moving heavy stones. The first wheels were certainly sections cut through logs. They were made of solid wood and were, of course, heavy. A straight stick of wood, or axle, joined two wheels together. Anyone who rode in a cart with such wheels would have a truly rough ride, and a noisy one. For a big solid wheel would certainly creak as it turned.

The pictures tell a part of the story of how the wheel grew up. They show, too, a very few of the many kinds of wheels in use today.

When, after Columbus discovered America, white explorers and settlers came to the New World, they found that some of the American Indians were highly civilized. But these Indians had no wheels. The wheel is a gift of the Old World to the New.

WHITE ELEPHANT Most elephants are brownish-gray. But every once in a while an elephant is born that is not that color. Instead it is a "dirty" white. Scientists call white elephants albinos. There are albinos among many kinds of animals. There are even white crows.

Long ago the idea grew in India and nearby lands that white elephants should be treated especially well. When a white elephant was found, it was usually given as a present to a ruler. The ruler of course took it. From then on he had to feed the elephant. He was expected to buy especially beautiful trappings for it, too. Having a white elephant cost a great deal, and the elephant did nothing in return.

Now, "It's a white elephant" is a common saying. Calling something you have "a white elephant" means, "I don't want this because it is hard to take care of. But it was a gift, and I have to keep it, at least for a while." When the time comes that a white elephant can be given away, it may be hard to find anyone who wants it.

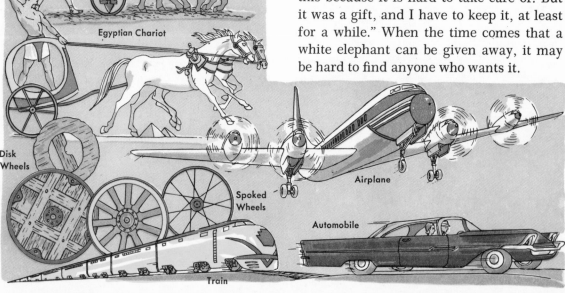

WHEELS THROUGH THE AGES

Sumerian Cart

Egyptian Chariot

Disk Wheels

Spoked Wheels

Airplane

Automobile

Train

Each year many people visit the White House, where the president of the United States lives.

WHITE HOUSE As soon as a man becomes the president of the United States, he moves into the big house shown in the picture. This is the White House. Of course, it is in Washington, D.C.

The White House was started when the United States was very, very young. An architect named James Hoban planned it. The first president to live in it was John Adams. When John Adams moved into the new house, it had not yet been finished. Mrs. Adams hung her washing in a big room that later became the East Room, the largest of all the many rooms in the building. In those days the White House was not white. Its walls were of gray sandstone. It was called the "President's Palace."

In 1814, during a war with the British, the President's Palace was badly damaged by fire. But it was soon rebuilt. It was painted white in 1817, when James Monroe was president. The paint hid the smoke stains that showed on some of the walls. The building has been white ever since.

Later presidents added more rooms to the White House. In time it came to have more than 60.

While Harry S. Truman was president, it was found that the building was in bad shape. The walls and ceilings were so weak that there was danger that the building would fall down. When the leg of a piano came through a ceiling into the room below, it was clear that something had to be done. Should the White House be torn down completely? No one wanted it greatly changed. This, then, is what was done:

A great steel framework was built inside the building to hold the walls and roof in place. Then the whole inside of the building was torn out and rebuilt.

The rebuilt White House was finished and ready for use again in 1952. It now has 107 rooms and 31 baths and lavatories. Some of the rooms are offices where the president works with his helpers. The main rooms were rebuilt just as they were before.

The best known of the White House rooms are the East Room, the Blue Room, the Green Room, the Red Room, and the State Dining Room. If the White House were a royal palace, the Blue Room would probably be the throne room. Here the president and the first lady greet the guests at state dinners. A hundred guests can be seated in the big State Dining Room.

Visitors are welcome at the White House. Every year about 1,000,000 people visit the home of the presidents of the United States. (See WASHINGTON, D.C.)

Wild Geraniums

Cardinal
Flower

Pasqueflowers

WILD FLOWERS Many of the flowers we raise in our gardens were brought to us from other lands. These flowers will not live unless we take care of them carefully. We must plant them and water them and pull up the weeds from around them. But we also have many flowers that take no work at all. These are our wild flowers. Most of them are native flowers. They were, that is, growing in America when white people first came here.

Some of our wild flowers bloom at one time of year, some at another. The wild geraniums, mallows, violets, and columbines in the pictures are spring flowers. Many spring flowers are found in woods. In woods made up of trees that lose their leaves in the fall, a great deal of sunshine can reach the ground in the spring before the trees leaf out. Woods often have regular carpets of flowers in early spring. After the trees leaf out there is too much shade for most kinds of flowers.

The other wild flowers in the pictures are summer and fall flowers. Many such flowers grow in meadows or along roadsides, where they get plenty of sunshine.

Mallows

Rose
Mallow

Some of our most beautiful wild flowers are in danger of disappearing. The showy lady's-slipper is one of them. We do not have to take care of our wild flowers as we do our garden flowers. But, if we do not want them to disappear, we must do all we can to keep from harming them.

We harm our wild flowers chiefly by picking too many of them. Flowers make seeds. If all the flowers of a plant are picked, the plant cannot make any seeds to start new plants. We also pick flowers carelessly. Sometimes we pull up a whole plant when we try to pick its flowers. Then, of course, it cannot produce other plants.

In the United States there are not nearly as many homes for wild flowers as there used to be. Much of the woodland and grassland has been turned into fields and gardens and orchards. Today the plants along many roadways are burned off. There is much less chance for wild flowers to grow there than there once was. Everyone should be careful not to disturb the wild flowers in the homes they still have left. (See BOTANY; CONSERVATION; FLOWER; FLOWER FAMILIES.)

Columbines

Gentians

Violets

William's bowmen helped win the Battle of Hastings.

WILLIAM THE CONQUEROR (1027-1087) The year 1066 is a very important date in English history. In that year Duke William of Normandy crossed the English Channel with about 5,000 men and conquered England by defeating Harold, the English king. The battle in which Harold was defeated is called the Battle of Hastings. William became the king of England. He is known as William the Conqueror.

William was the son of Duke Robert of Normandy, who died when William was only eight years old. As duke, William ruled a small but powerful province that is now a part of France. Normandy was no easy land to rule. The boy ruler soon found out that ruling well is hard. But by the time he had grown to manhood he had become a strong ruler. Even his enemies admired him. An enemy once said that no knight under heaven was William's peer.

It may seem strange in these days of armies with millions of men that William, with only 5,000 men, conquered a country! Actually, Harold seemed to have the greater army but William won partly because he had horsemen and powerful archers, and partly because Harold's men were tired. They had just defeated another invader. William was not quite 40 years old when he conquered England.

The new Norman ruler brought French customs and the French language to Britain. He brought the idea of great castles and cathedrals. Some of his ideas were very startling to the English peasants.

In spite of some attempts to overthrow him, he built up a strong nation. He made not only the noblemen but all the peasants swear loyalty to him.

In William's reign we find the beginning of trial by jury. In the *Domesday Book* William kept a record of all the lands of England. These records helped him tell what taxes each landowner should pay. To be sure that his records were right, he gathered together in every district a group of 12 men to check the records. Two centuries later similar groups became juries.

The Battle of Hastings was one of the most important battles in history. It is interesting to try to imagine how different history would have been if William had been defeated. (See ANGLO-SAXONS; ARMY; ENGLAND'S HISTORY; ENGLISH LANGUAGE; HISTORY.)

WILL-O'-THE-WISP On summer evenings a patch of light may move about over a marsh. Such a patch of light is called the will-o'-the-wisp. Other names for it are friar's lantern, jack-o'-lantern, and Robin Goodfellow. Another name, *ignis fatuus*, means "foolish fire."

There are many superstitions about "foolish fire." Some people say that the lights are given off by candles carried by ghosts. Some say that marsh sprites are luring people to their death in the marshes. Some say that a mischievous elf, Robin Goodfellow, is playing tricks.

Actually the patches of light usually come from the slow burning of a gas formed in marshes. Sometimes the lights come from rotting wood, which often glows in the dark. We say that it is phosphorescent. The lights may also come from tiny insects that glow like fireflies.

"He is following a will-o'-the-wisp" is a common saying. It means, "He is following an idea that seems better than it is—one that will not get him anywhere."

WIND As almost everyone knows, wind is moving air. Sometimes the wind is gentle. Sometimes it is strong. When the weatherman says that the wind is gentle, he means that the air is moving slowly. When he says that the wind is strong, he means that the air is moving fast.

A wind gets its name from the direction it comes from. A wind from the north is a north wind. And one coming from the southeast is a southeast wind.

Wind has much to do with weather. Warm weather often comes with a south wind. A north wind may bring a cold wave. East winds are likely to bring cloudy skies, and west winds fair weather. A weatherman must know about the wind before he can tell us what kind of weather we are going to have.

The weatherman has instruments that measure the speed of the wind accurately. But anyone can measure it roughly for himself by using a chart like the one below.

IF:	THE WIND IS BLOWING:
smoke goes straight up,	less than 1 mile an hour.
the leaves on trees are rustling a little,	from 1 to 7 miles an hour.
flags blow straight out but no branches move,	from 8 to 12 miles an hour.
small branches sway and paper is blown about,	from 13 to 18 miles an hour.
small trees are swaying and there are whitecaps on bodies of water,	from 19 to 24 miles an hour.
umbrellas are hard to hold and large branches are moving,	from 25 to 38 miles an hour.
trees are uprooted and big branches break,	over 39 miles an hour.

Sousaphone

Saxophones

Trombone

WIND INSTRUMENTS

To make a sound something must vibrate. Something must, that is, move back and forth very fast. In wind instruments the musical sound is made by the vibration of air inside the instruments.

All the instruments shown in the pictures on these pages are wind instruments. In all of them it is air that vibrates. But there are different ways of setting the air inside a wind instrument to vibrating.

A flute is played by blowing across a small hole near one end. The sound is made just as a sound can be made by blowing across the top of an "empty" small-mouthed bottle. As the air is blown across the opening it sets the air inside to vibrating. The piccolo, the flageolet, and the fife are other instruments played in the same way. They are all slender, rather short instruments. They are said to come from an ancient wind instrument called the pipes of Pan, which had several tubes.

A clarinet has a thin, flat piece of cane in its mouthpiece. This is called a reed. The player blows into the mouthpiece and sets the reed to vibrating. The movement of the reed then sets the air in the clarinet to vibrating. The saxophone is another instrument that has a reed in its mouthpiece. The oboe, the bassoon, and the English horn are double reed instruments.

A trombone player presses his lips against the mouthpiece of his instrument. He then makes his lips vibrate, and they set the air inside the trombone to vibrating. The cornet, trumpet, French horn, and tuba are all played in this way.

A common whistle is a wind instrument of a kind, although the sound a whistle makes is not usually very musical. Even a whistle with a pleasant sound would not

Oboes

English Horns

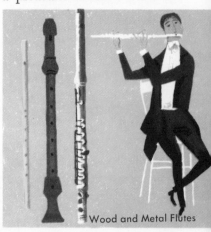

Wood and Metal Flutes

be a good musical instrument for it can produce only one note. You could not possibly play a tune on a whistle. Wind instruments can produce many notes.

The note a column of air gives off when it vibrates depends on how big around the column of air is and how long it is. In the pipes of Pan there are tubes of different lengths. The player can therefore play several notes. In the wind instruments of today there is only one tube, but the player has a way of making the tube longer or shorter. There isn't, of course, any way he can make it bigger around or smaller. In the flute and its family of instruments there are openings along the tube. The length of tube that counts is from the "blow hole" to the first opening. A flute player keeps his fingers busy opening and closing tiny "doors" while he plays, so that the flute will play different notes.

A trombone has a movable tube that slides in and out of the other part of the instrument. The player makes the trombone give off different notes by sliding the movable tube in and out.

In a trumpet and the instruments much like it, there are valves, or stops. A player presses down these valves as he plays. The valves open and close off sections of the tube so that the length of the column of air keeps changing.

A bassoon cannot make as high a note as a flute. A tuba cannot make as high a note as a trumpet. The bassoon and the

Clarinet and Bass Clarinet

tuba produce low notes. Their tubes are big and long. If a tuba's tube were stretched out straight, it would be very hard to hold and it would get in the way of all the players near by. To get great length without taking up too much space, the tube is curved around and around.

The flutes, clarinets, oboes, English horns, and bassoons of an orchestra are often spoken of as the wood winds. They are usually made of wood, but not always. Some of the best flutes are made of silver.

Trumpets, cornets, French horns, trombones, and tubas are often called brasses. They are made of metal, usually of brass.

All full orchestras have both wood winds and brasses. Some bands have only brasses. Brasses along with drums give just the right kind of music for marching. (See BAND; MUSIC; MUSICAL INSTRUMENTS; ORCHESTRA.)

Bassoons

Cornets

French Horn

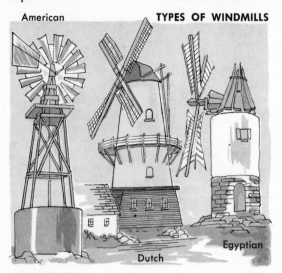

American   TYPES OF WINDMILLS

Dutch

Egyptian

WINDMILL Centuries ago men learned how to harness the wind so that it would help them. For the sea they built ships with sails. On land they built windmills.

A windmill is a big wheel with blades. It is mounted high in the air so that its blades will catch the wind. The wind makes the wheel turn. The turning wheel runs a machine of some kind. It may be a pump, a flour mill, or a small electric generator.

Wind does not always blow from the same direction. There has to be some way of keeping a windmill turned so that the wind will strike it at the right angle. In some cases there is a weather vane. Or there may be a little windmill that helps get the big wheel into the right position.

The Netherlands is famous for its windmills. Much of the land there is low. It is below the level of the sea. Pumps must be kept running to keep the land from being flooded. For a long time almost all the pumping was done by windmills. Now windmills are not nearly so important. Most of the pumping is now done by gasoline engines and electric motors. Of course, a windmill is not of any use unless there is enough wind to turn it. Gasoline engines and electric motors are more dependable.

In the United States windmills were once a common sight on farms. The creak of the big wheel was a well-known sound. The windmills were used chiefly to pump water for farm animals. Now they are scarce except on the western plains where there is a great sweep for the wind. On most American farms windmills have made way for gasoline engines and electric motors just as they have in the Netherlands. (See NETHERLANDS.)

WIND TUNNEL As an airplane flies, the air flows past it in a complicated way. The flow of the air has a great deal to do with how fast the plane can fly. When an airplane builder has an idea for a new type of airplane, he needs to know exactly how the air would flow past it. He makes a model and tests it in a wind tunnel. A wind tunnel is a big tube or room through which great fans send a strong wind. The winds in wind tunnels reproduce the same conditions the plane would meet in moving through the air at very high speeds. The airplane builder can see how his model acts in the wind tunnel and can tell if design changes are needed. (See AIRPLANES.)

WINTER SPORTS To many people summer is playtime and winter is work time. But there are many winter sports. Some of these winter sports are becoming more and more popular. The pictures show some of those that are best liked.

Skating is an old sport—at least several centuries old. In England the first skates were made of thin pieces of bone that could be fastened to boots by straps. The runners are made of steel now.

Some skaters work for speed. There are skating races in many places. Others like figure skating better. Figure skating is fancy skating. Skating in a figure 8 is one of the simpler things that a figure skater learns to do.

Skating is an important part of another winter sport—ice hockey. Ice hockey is often played indoors on artificial ice arenas. But it is played out of doors, too. The game is to knock a little rubber disk called a puck into a goal net.

Sometimes skaters fasten sails to their backs. Wind blowing against the sails moves skaters fast over the ice. Skating with the help of sails is called skate sailing.

Almost every boy or girl in the colder parts of the United States has played with a sled. Sleds are wonderful for coasting down snow-covered hills. So are toboggans. Toboggans are built of long strips of wood curled up at one end. They were first made by American Indians.

Bobsleds are made of two single sleds with a platform joining them. Bobsledding down a long steep hill is exciting.

Tramping over the snow in the crisp cold air of a winter day is fun. Snowshoes make walking over snow rather easy. They keep their wearers from sinking down into the snow. The Indians were using snowshoes when white settlers first came to America.

Skis also help their wearers travel over snow. They were probably first used in Norway. Wearing a pair of skis is much like having a toboggan on each foot. Skiing down slopes takes a great deal of skill. In many places special slopes called ski jumps have been built. Ski jumpers make wonderful leaps through the air from the lower end of these jumps.

Iceboats look much like the sailboats that sail in water. But they are built with runners for traveling over ice.

The game called curling comes from Scotland. Four-man teams play it with heavy "stones" made of polished granite. Each stone has a handle for use in sending it scooting over the ice toward the mark. Each player has a broom for sweeping the ice in front of a teammate's stone. The sweeping has a great deal to do with the way the stone travels.

The Olympic games are held every four years. The games used to be held only in the summer. But now there are winter Olympics, too. The sports in the winter games are figure and speed skating, ice hockey, bobsledding, skiing, and sometimes curling. (See HOCKEY; ICE SKATING.)

SOME FAVORITE WINTER SPORTS

Skiing

Figure Skating

Ice Boating

Tobogganing

WISCONSIN This Great Lakes state is neither a large nor a crowded one. Wisconsin is the "Dairyland of America," but farming is not the only important work there. Fewer people live on farms than in cities. Wisconsin is a leading manufacturing state. It is also a much-enjoyed vacation land. Glaciers tore down the mountains of 25 million years ago. They left behind them a land of ridges, low rolling hills, valleys, and beautiful lakes.

Dairying is a good branch of farming in Wisconsin, where summers are not long and hot and much of the land is rolling or hilly. Most Wisconsin dairy farmers use many mechanical helpers to get big milk production. Milk is sent to city people or to dairy plants to be made into cheese, butter, and condensed or powdered milk.

Wisconsin cheese factories make more cheese than is made in any other state. The bulk of the cheese is now made in modern plants. In these one may see great wheels or bricks of cheese aging on racks in cold rooms. Cheese scrapers trim off the blue-green mold from the cheeses. Wisconsin Swiss, brick, and other cheeses are sold all over the United States and in foreign lands.

Wisconsin's factories turn out diesel engines, giant turbines, auto frames, pasteurizing machines, tractors, beer, paper, and other well-known products. The big plants are in the cities along or near Lake Michigan between Green Bay and Kenosha. But there are factories in towns all over the state. Power plants on the Wisconsin and other rivers furnish electricity.

More of the big industries are in Milwaukee and its suburbs than in any other city. Milwaukee is one of the busiest ports on the Great Lakes. Much has been done over the years to make it bigger and better. At its docks are mountains of coal, pig iron and scrap, tall grain elevators, oil storage tanks, and warehouses. Foreign ships come to Milwaukee's port. With the Great Lakes-St. Lawrence Seaway, more and larger ships are expected to come to Milwaukee. The city of Superior, on Lake Superior, has the world's biggest ore dock.

The story of white men in Wisconsin begins with Jean Nicolet, the French explorer. He arrived at Green Bay in 1634 and claimed the land for France. Later the British had control until it became American territory. In 1848 Wisconsin was made a state. Madison is the capital.

Wisconsin seemed to have room for everybody. Southerners pushed up the Mississippi to the lead mining areas. Miners from England quarried the stone around Mineral Point. It was from miners digging into hillsides, the way badgers burrow holes into the ground, that Wisconsin became known as the "Badger State." Farmers from the East, Scots, Welshmen, and Irish poured into the state.

Germans came to the area around Milwaukee as farmers, tanners, brewers, and managers of small factories. Swiss founded cheese factories. Scandinavians came to work in the northern pine forests and iron mines. Poles, Italians, and others came later. These people all helped to make Wisconsin. They and their children and their children's children are all good Americans helping to use Wisconsin's riches well.

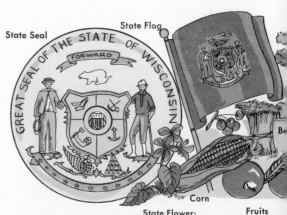

State Seal   State Flag

GREAT SEAL OF THE STATE OF WISCONSIN

FORWARD

Corn

State Flower: Violet   Fruits

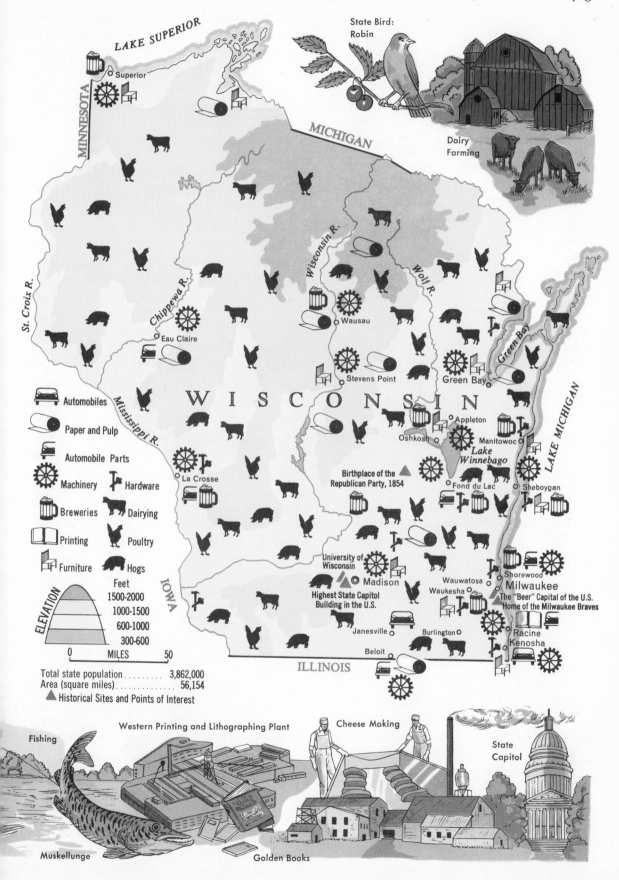

State Bird: Robin

Dairy Farming

LAKE SUPERIOR

MINNESOTA

Superior

MICHIGAN

Wisconsin R.

Wolf R.

Chippewa R.

St. Croix R.

Eau Claire

Wausau

Green Bay

Stevens Point

Green Bay

W I S C O N S I N

Mississippi R.

LAKE MICHIGAN

Appleton

Oshkosh

Manitowoc

La Crosse

Lake Winnebago

Birthplace of the Republican Party, 1854

Fond du Lac

Sheboygan

Automobiles

Paper and Pulp

Automobile Parts

Machinery   **Hardware**

Breweries   **Dairying**

Printing   **Poultry**

Furniture   **Hogs**

University of Wisconsin

Madison

Highest State Capitol Building in the U.S.

Wauwatosa

Waukesha

Shorewood

Milwaukee

The "Beer" Capital of the U.S. Home of the Milwaukee Braves

IOWA

Feet
1500-2000
1000-1500
600-1000
300-600

ELEVATION

0   MILES   50

Racine
Kenosha

Janesville

Burlington

Beloit

ILLINOIS

Total state population......... 3,862,000
Area (square miles)............. 56,154
▲ Historical Sites and Points of Interest

Fishing

Western Printing and Lithographing Plant

Cheese Making

State Capitol

GOLDEN BOOKS

Muskellunge

Golden Books

Wombats make very affectionate pets.

WOMBAT The wombat is about the size of a big dog but it looks more like a small bear. It has stout legs, long hair, and almost no tail. It is, however, not at all closely related to the bears. Strange as it seems, it is a much closer relative of the kangaroo. Like the kangaroo it is a pouched mammal, or marsupial. It is found, along with most of the pouched mammals, only in Australia and nearby Tasmania.

One wombat baby is born at a time. The mother carries it in her pouch for seven or eight months. Then it can live on its own.

Wombats live in tunnels they dig in the ground. Their nail-like claws are excellent tools for digging. Some of their tunnels are 100 feet long. A wombat usually stays in its tunnel all day. It does most of its food-hunting during the night.

Wombats eat grass, tree bark, and roots of different kinds. They have teeth that are much like the teeth of woodchucks and other rodents. The teeth grow all the time and are therefore never worn down.

The natives of Australia like the meat of the wombat very much. In some tribes there are rules which tell exactly how a hunter must divide a wombat he catches. His mother gets one certain part, his mother-in-law another, and each of his other relatives a share, too. (See AUSTRALIA; POUCHED MAMMALS.)

WOOD Many plants have soft stems. But trees and shrubs and some vines have stems made mostly of wood.

All plants, like all animals, are built of cells. Wood is made of a special kind of cell that has thick, strong walls. In most plants with woody stems a new layer of wood is made every year. It is like a cuff on the outside of the older wood. A layer of fast-growing cells called the cambium makes the new wood. It is the innermost layer of the bark.

Wood cells when they are first made are filled with living material. But they lose it very soon. They form hollow tubes through which water travels. In time the older wood cells toward the center of the stem become a kind of dumping ground. The plant sends some of its waste materials there. These waste materials fill up the cells. They may stain the wood dark. They make it tough and strong. This older and tougher wood is called heartwood. The newer wood on the outside is called sapwood. Only sapwood can carry water.

Not all the wood cells in a stem are the same size. Those made in the spring are usually bigger than those made in the fall. When a woody stem is cut across, the wood of each year in most cases shows as a ring. In each ring the cells go from large to small. The big cells made each spring are

METHODS OF SAWING   **BOARD CUTS**

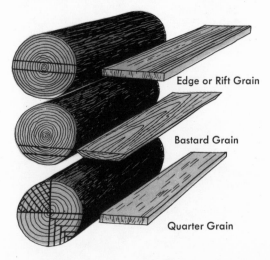

Edge or Rift Grain

Bastard Grain

Quarter Grain

next to the small cells that were made the fall before. The difference in the size of the cells makes the rings easy to count. Counting the rings in a tree trunk tells us how old the tree was when it was cut down.

Although bushes and many vines have woody stems, almost all the wood we use comes from trees. The trunks of some trees are used for telephone poles and piles for foundations. Many go to sawmills and are cut into railroad ties, fence posts, and lumber. The men at the sawmills know just how to do the cutting. They can cut a tree trunk so that the different sizes of cells make beautiful patterns in the wood. The picture shows three common ways of cutting planks from tree trunks.

Some kinds of wood are much harder than others. Mahogany, walnut, and oak are three very hard woods. They are especially good for furniture. Red spruce and Douglas fir are soft woods. They make good lumber for building.

Much wood is made into some other material before it is used. Acres of forest are cut down every day for making paper and plastics and rayon. In parts of the world, moreover, wood is still being used as the cave men used it—for fuel. (See BARK; CELL; FORESTS AND FORESTRY; FUELS; LUMBERING; PETRIFIED WOOD; SHRUBS; TREES; VINES.)

WOOD CARVING For thousands of years people have carved beautiful figures and designs out of wood. Wood carving is one of the oldest arts. It is probably even older than carving in stone, for wood is easier to carve. Even hard wood is softer than most stone. No one can tell surely when wood carving began, because wood in time rots away. Insects such as termites eat it, too. It is a safe guess, however, that some of the cave men carved wooden handles for their knives.

Even though we are sure we do not have any samples of the earliest wood carving, we do have some very old samples. One of them is a figure called "The Village Chief." It was made in Egypt about 5,000 years ago. This statue was carved in wood. It was then covered with plaster and painted. The eyes were inlaid and rimmed with copper.

Down through the ages many of the figures and designs carved in wood have been painted. Some of them are still painted today. But now many wood carvers think that the wood itself is so beautiful that they do not cover it up with paint.

Wood carving was at its best four or five hundred years ago. The woodwork inside the great castles and cathedrals of that time was usually beautifully carved. Statues of characters in the Bible were in great demand for the cathedrals, too. In the heyday of sailing vessels, each vessel had a figurehead. Here was another good opportunity for wood carvers. Today people prefer furniture that is simple and walls that are plain. Most of the wood carvers of today work on small figures, as the man in the picture below is doing. The boy beside him in the picture is whittling. Whittling is the simplest kind of wood carving. (See ARTS; SCULPTURE.)

A Skilled Wood Carver Teaching His Son

Red-headed
Woodpecker

Flicker

Yellow-bellied
Sapsucker

WOODPECKER The rat-ta-tat-tat of a woodpecker is a well-known sound. The bird makes the sound by pecking at a tree or a roof or a telephone pole. It may be drilling holes in wood to get something to eat. It may be digging out a nest. It may be drumming out a song to its mate.

There are woodpeckers in almost every land. In the United States there are more than 20 kinds. The pictures show a few of them. The ivory-billed woodpecker is the country's rarest bird.

Woodpeckers have strong, sharp bills. Their tails are short and stubby with sharp points at the end. Most woodpeckers have four toes on each foot. Two point forward and two backward.

Woodpeckers eat chiefly insects and insect eggs. To get insects that live in wood, they hold fast with their toes, brace themselves with their tails, and peck on the wood in front of them. They use their tongues to pull out any insects they find. Most woodpeckers have long sticky tongues with sharp points at the end.

Flickers, unlike most other kinds of woodpeckers, are often seen on the ground. They eat enormous numbers of ants.

Woodpeckers of most kinds are very welcome in our parks and forests. They eat insects that harm trees. Only a few are not welcome. The unwanted ones are the sapsuckers. As their name tells, they drink sap from trees. (See BIRDS.)

Ivory-billed Woodpecker

WOOL Of all the fibers that can be made into cloth, wool was probably first used. No one knows when the making of woolen cloth began. It began before the days of written history. No one knows, either, who first found that wool can be woven into cloth. The discovery, whoever made it, was a wonderful discovery.

Wool fibers are the curly hairs that make up the thick coats of sheep. On each fiber of wool tiny scales lap over one another like the scales of a fish. The scales can be seen when a bit of wool is examined under a microscope.

There are at least 200 kinds of sheep. Some are large sheep and some are small. There are sheep with long wool and sheep with short wool. Some have fine wool and some have coarse wool. Most people agree that the best wool of all is the wool that comes from Merino sheep.

Sheep of the same kind do not always give the same grade of wool. The grade of wool depends on many different things. The health of the sheep is one. The kind of food the sheep have had is another. What the weather has been is a third. Still another is the age of the sheep the wool is cut from. The best wool comes from young sheep. "Lamb's wool" comes from a sheep's first shearing. As soon as it is sheared, a sheep begins growing a new heavy coat.

In early times all woolen cloth was made at home. The men sheared the sheep. The women straightened out the fibers. "Cards" were often used to straighten out the fibers. The cards were flat pieces of wood with wires in them like the bristles of brushes. Straightening out wool fibers is still called "carding" the wool. After the fibers were straightened, the women twisted them into threads, or yarn. At first spindles turned by hand were used. Later the spinning wheel was invented. After the yarn was spun, the women wove it into cloth. Sometimes the yarn was dyed before weaving. Some weavers dyed their cloth after it was woven.

In some places much spinning and weaving is still done by hand. But in the United States most of the work is carried on in factories called woolen mills.

Of course, the first step in making woolen goods is still shearing the sheep. On big sheep ranches the shearing is often done with electric clipping machines. On small farms it is still done with hand shears. In a very few minutes a sheep's wool lies in a heap. The whole coat of wool of a full-grown sheep is called a fleece. The fleeces are rolled up and are packed in bales. The bales of wool are then sent on their way to market.

At the woolen mill the wool is sorted. Burs are pulled out. Then it is thoroughly washed. There is sure to be dirt and grease in it. The clean, wet wool is sent next to a drying room. When it is dry, it is white and soft and fluffy.

The wool next goes to a carding room. Here the fibers are straightened out and gathered up into loose "ropes." In the best woolen cloth only the longer wool fibers are used. They are separated from the shorter ones in a combing machine.

The wool next goes to the spinning room. Here machines twist it into yarn. It is now ready to be woven into cloth.

Most wool is dyed. It may be dyed before it is carded, before it is spun, before it is woven, or after it is made into cloth.

Felt is cloth that is not spun or woven. The fibers are simply steamed and pressed together. The scales on the tangled fibers hold them together.

The hair of some other animals is so much like wool that it is often called wool. Among these animals are the alpaca, the llama, the vicuña, and some kinds of goats. Camel's hair is also much like wool. It can be made into beautiful soft cloth.

Of course, not all wool goes into clothing. Carpets, rugs, and blankets are a few of the other uses of wool.

The United States produces many millions of pounds of wool a year. But it needs still more, and so it buys wool from other countries. Australia has much wool to sell. It leads the world in wool production. (See CARPETS AND RUGS; SHEEP; SPINNING AND WEAVING.)

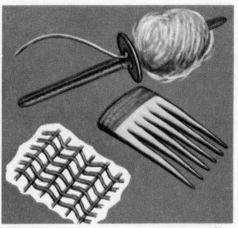

Early man combed, spun, and wove wool.

Kaiser Wilhelm II

Assassination of Archduke Ferdinand

Sinking of the "Lusitania"

Use of Tanks

Germans in Retreat

WORLD WAR I The bullet that started World War I was fired by a young student from Serbia, once a country but now a part of Yugoslavia. The bullet killed Archduke Francis Ferdinand, the heir to the throne of Austria-Hungary. Exactly one month later, on July 28, 1914, Austria-Hungary declared war on Serbia, and World War I began. By the time it ended, 60,000,000 men had taken up arms, and about 8,500,000 had been killed.

For many years before the war started, trouble had been brewing among the nations of Europe. The new factories that were springing up in Europe created a struggle among the nations for world markets and for sources of raw materials. The race for colonies caused trouble, too. France and Britain grabbed most of Africa, causing great anger in Germany. Austria-Hungary was trying to get a port on the Aegean Sea, but the countries of Serbia and Montenegro stood in the way. All of the larger nations of Europe built up their armies and promised to aid their allies.

Within a few days after Austria-Hungary declared war on Serbia, other nations of Europe jumped into the war on one side or the other. The lineup of major nations had Austria-Hungary, Germany, Turkey, and Bulgaria on one side. This group was called the Central Powers. On the other side were the Allies: France, Great Britain, Russia, Belgium, and Italy.

Germany dominated the fighting in the early days of the war. German troops stormed through Belgium and invaded France. They got to within a few miles of Paris before they were halted by the forces of France and Britain. In the east, Germany and Austria-Hungary swept through Poland and advanced into Russia. Italy entered the war in 1915 on the side of the Allies. Italy's entry forced the Central Powers to fight on the southern front.

After some early victories, Germany's armies were brought to a standstill. For months the war on land dragged on with neither side able to win.

At sea, the superior navy of Great Britain was in command. The German warships did not venture beyond the North Sea. Finally, however, the Germans turned to submarine warfare. They believed that if the submarines could prevent supplies from reaching Britain and France, the Allies would be forced to surrender. But many of the ships that were carrying supplies to the Allies were American ships. After a number of American ships had been sunk by German submarines, the United States entered the war on the side of the Allies on April 6, 1917.

The entry of the United States helped turn the tide in favor of the Allies. About a year later, German, Austrian, and Turkish armies were in retreat throughout Europe. A truce ending the war was signed November 11, 1918, in a railroad car in northern France. It was "Armistice Day."

World War I greatly changed the map of Europe, but it solved almost none of the problems which had caused the war. The German, Austrian, and Turkish empires shrank to small size. New countries, among them Czechoslovakia, Poland, and Yugoslavia, came into being. The League of Nations was created in an attempt to prevent future wars. But only 21 years later, the world was once again at war.

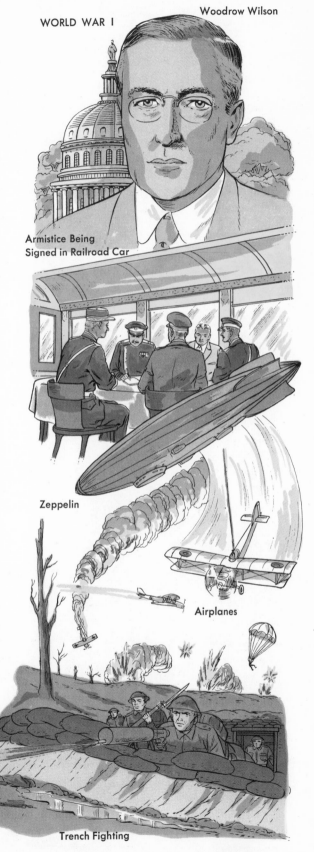

WORLD WAR I

Woodrow Wilson

Armistice Being Signed in Railroad Car

Zeppelin

Airplanes

Shellholes

Trench Fighting

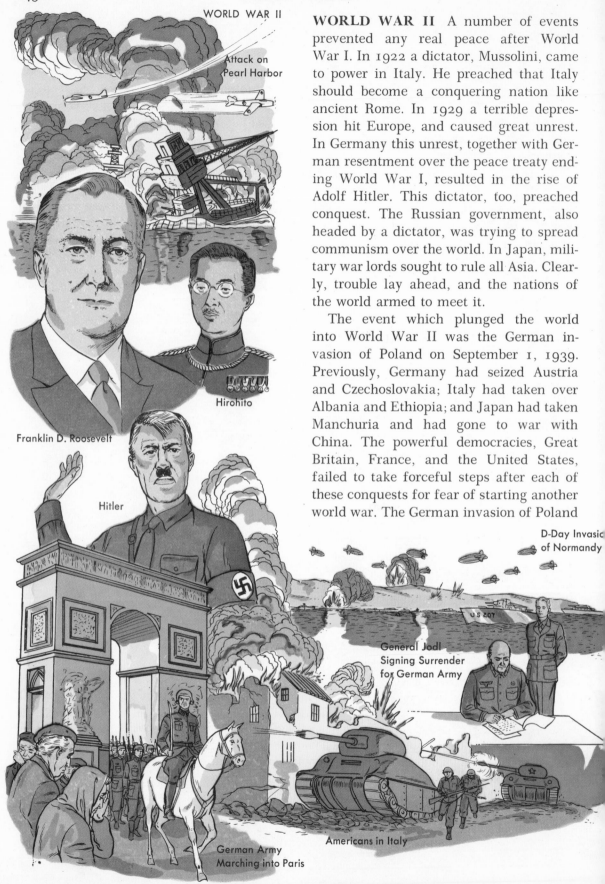

WORLD WAR II

Attack on Pearl Harbor

Hirohito

Franklin D. Roosevelt

Hitler

D-Day Invasion of Normandy

General Jodl Signing Surrender for German Army

German Army Marching into Paris

Americans in Italy

WORLD WAR II A number of events prevented any real peace after World War I. In 1922 a dictator, Mussolini, came to power in Italy. He preached that Italy should become a conquering nation like ancient Rome. In 1929 a terrible depression hit Europe, and caused great unrest. In Germany this unrest, together with German resentment over the peace treaty ending World War I, resulted in the rise of Adolf Hitler. This dictator, too, preached conquest. The Russian government, also headed by a dictator, was trying to spread communism over the world. In Japan, military war lords sought to rule all Asia. Clearly, trouble lay ahead, and the nations of the world armed to meet it.

The event which plunged the world into World War II was the German invasion of Poland on September 1, 1939. Previously, Germany had seized Austria and Czechoslovakia; Italy had taken over Albania and Ethiopia; and Japan had taken Manchuria and had gone to war with China. The powerful democracies, Great Britain, France, and the United States, failed to take forceful steps after each of these conquests for fear of starting another world war. The German invasion of Poland convinced the British and French leaders that the time to stop Hitler had come. They declared war on Germany.

In the early months of the war, Hitler's troops swept through Poland, Denmark, Norway, the Netherlands, Belgium, and Luxembourg. France surrendered on June 22, 1940, just a few days after Italy joined the war on Germany's side. Great Britain endured terrible air raids and waited for an invasion that never came.

In the early stages of the war, the people of the United States had a great deal of sympathy for Britain and France. Under the terms of a law called the Lend-Lease Act, the United States shipped war supplies to Britain and later to the Soviet Union.

Exactly one year after France fell, Germany invaded the Soviet Union. Many people consider this invasion Germany's first serious military mistake. The war against the Soviet Union drained much of Germany's manpower and equipment.

The United States was actively drawn into the war as a result of the Japanese sneak attack on Pearl Harbor, Hawaii, on Dec. 7, 1941. The next day, the United States declared war on Japan, and a few days later on Germany and Italy.

War equipment in enormous quantities was sent to the English and to the Russians from the United States. As the flood of weapons increased, the United States, British, and Russian armed forces began to take the offensive. North Africa was recaptured from the Germans by the British, who then, together with the Americans, invaded Italy. The Russians began to push the Germans back. Normandy, in France, was invaded by the Allies on June 6, 1944. The war ended in Europe when the Germans surrendered on May 7, 1945.

After suffering heavy losses in the Pacific, the United States began to take the attack. The Japanese were pushed back from New Guinea, the Philippines, and other islands. Finally, even Japan itself was under attack from Allied planes. After two atom bombs were dropped, Japan surrendered on August 10, 1945.

The destruction in World War II was greater than any the world had ever known. While most of the democratic nations had not been conquered, they had suffered greatly. Soon after the end of the war, the United Nations was organized to try to make sure that no such war would ever be fought again. (See UNITED NATIONS.)

Atom Bomb

Super Fortress

Flag Raising on Iwo Jima

Infantryman Using Bazooka

General MacArthur Signing the Japanese Surrender with Shigemitsu

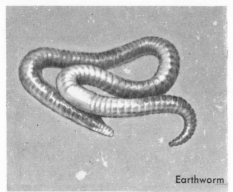
Earthworm

WORMS To most people the word "worm" means something ugly and perhaps even dangerous. Some worms *are* ugly, and some cause diseases. But there are beautiful worms, too, and there are helpful ones.

Some worms are flat; some are round; some have bodies divided into sections, or segments. Some live in water; others live in the ground; and still others live inside the bodies of other animals. But worms are all alike in certain ways. They are slender. They have soft bodies. And they are legless or nearly so.

The most helpful worm is the common earthworm. It is a great help in making soil rich. And it is good bait for fish.

The only really beautiful worms live in the sea. Some of them are called sea jewels or sea flowers. Many of them build little chimneys of sand or lime around themselves. Some sea worms have gills which look like tiny colored plumes.

The planaria is a flatworm. Scientists sometimes use this little worm to show what wonderful powers some animals have of growing new parts. If a planaria is cut into two pieces, each piece will grow into a whole worm.

The tapeworm is one of the worms that does harm. It lives inside the bodies of other animals. Many pet dogs have to be taken to a veterinary because they have tapeworms. The hookworm is another worm that lives inside other animals. It may live inside people and cause hookworm disease. Another dangerous worm is sometimes found in pork. Pork should always be well cooked before it is eaten.

Some animals are called worms by mistake. Most of them are young insects. The caterpillar of a butterfly looks much like a worm, but in time it changes to a creature with wings. The babies of some other insects look even more like worms. But young insects soon lose their wormlike look. Worms look like worms all their lives. (See BUTTERFLIES AND MOTHS; EARTHWORM; INSECTS; INVERTEBRATES.)

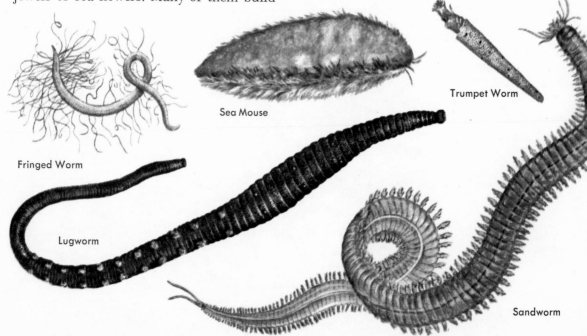

Fringed Worm

Sea Mouse

Trumpet Worm

Lugworm

Sandworm

WRIGHT, WILBUR (1867-1912) and **ORVILLE** (1871-1948) It was Dec. 14, 1903. The Wright brothers were at Kitty Hawk, N. C., ready to try out the airplane they had built. The wind blowing across the sand was cold but not strong. Wilbur and Orville tossed a coin to see who would make the first try. Wilbur won. He got in the plane and started the engine. The plane started along the track they had built for it. It left the ground, but something went wrong. It stayed in the air just 2½ seconds. The brothers decided that this unsuccessful flight did not count.

Three days later the plane was ready for another test. This time it was Orville's turn. The wind was rather strong — about 27 miles an hour. The engine was started, and the plane moved slowly down the track. After it had gone 40 feet it rose off the ground. Wilbur ran along beside it. It flew 120 feet in 12 seconds.

The brothers were very happy. For more than 2,000 years people had wanted to fly and had tried to find a way. At last someone had succeeded.

It was not the first time anyone had traveled by air. Balloons had carried people. But travel by balloon was floating, not flying. Gliders had carried people through the air, too. But a glider's flight was controlled largely by air currents. Here for the first time a heavier-than-air machine carrying a person had risen into the air and flown by its own power.

The same day—Dec. 17—Orville made another flight and Wilbur made two. The longest was one of Wilbur's. It lasted 59 seconds. The plane flew 852 feet.

Wilbur and Orville Wright ran a bicycle shop in Dayton, O. They were trying out their plane at Kitty Hawk, far away from home, because the United States Weather Bureau had told them that the winds there would be good for their experiments.

It was not just luck that the Wright brothers succeeded in flying. They had spent years studying and experimenting.

The Wright brothers got their plane into the air.

Wilbur Wright was born near Millville, Ind. Orville was born in Dayton. Their father was a minister. The boys did not even graduate from high school. But they were great readers. They liked to tinker with machines, too. The two brothers liked bicycles so much that they decided to set up a bicycle shop.

In their reading they came upon many accounts of experiments with flying. They talked about why the experiments had failed. After four years of reading and talking they thought it was time to try their hand. They started with gliders. They first built a five-foot glider. They flew it as a kite and watched it carefully. Even when they built a glider big enough to carry a man they first flew it as a kite. By this time they had chosen Kitty Hawk as a place to experiment. They planned to fly for hours there in their glider. But they made only a dozen free glider flights, all very short.

The brothers knew that before they could build an airplane they would need to know a great deal about air pressure. They built a wind tunnel to study it. They knew they would need a light, strong engine. They built one. They knew they would need better propellers than any that could be bought. They worked out a new design. And their careful work and study paid.

Honors were heaped upon the brothers. A beautiful monument to them now stands on Kill Devil Hill at Kitty Hawk. (See AIRPLANES; AIRPORTS; AIRWAYS; HELICOPTER; TRANSPORTATION.)

Cave Man Drawing Picture on Cave Wall

WRITING It is hard to think that writing had a beginning. But there was a time when there was no such thing as an alphabet. And there was a time, long before that, when no one could read or write at all.

We do not have to go back to early times to find some peoples just learning to read and write. In the farming villages of one part of Turkey, for example, reading and writing are both rather new. It has not been very long since the Turkish government set up schools in these villages to teach both the grownups and the children to read and write. The government introduced a simpler alphabet, too, so that reading and writing would be easier.

But seeing people learn to write now does not help us imagine how writing began. Learning how to write from people who know how is not at all like inventing a way of writing when no one in the world has ever written a single word.

Writing began thousands of years ago— long before there were any pens or pencils or paper or ink. The first writing we know anything about is on the walls of some of the caves of the cave men. It was written during the time that we call the Old Stone Age. The writing is made up entirely of pictures of animals. Of course the pictures might have been drawn just for decora-

tion. If they were, they are not writing. But the caves were dark, and many of the pictures are on the ceilings where they do not show very well. Probably some of them were records of the animals killed during a good hunting season. Probably some were messages to whatever gods the cave men believed in; they were prayers for good hunting.

Even if the pictures in the caves are not writing, the earliest writing was certainly picture writing. Every kind of writing that anyone knows about came in the beginning from picture writing.

In the early days of America the Indians were still writing in picture writing. The picture at the bottom of the page is a record written by an Indian. The record tells that a party of white men had camped near by. Eight soldiers armed with guns had one campfire. An officer and five other

American Indian Picture Story on Animal Skin

white men had another campfire. The party had two Indian guides, who had a campfire of their own. The leader of the guides was Pouncing Hawk. The Indians had been hunting and had caught a prairie chicken and a turtle.

For a simple record picture writing did well enough. But picture writing can tell only a very simple story. No one could write in picture writing a sentence like this: The English language is a hard language for foreigners to learn.

Several thousand years ago the Egyptians wrote in a kind of writing called "hieroglyphic." "Hieroglyphic" means "sacred writing cut in stone." The Greeks gave it this long name when they first saw some of it. But not all of it is sacred, and it is not all cut in stone. A great deal of it is written in ink on papyrus. Papyrus was somewhat like paper. The Egyptians made it from a plant which grew on the banks of the Nile.

This is "Jack and Jill" as the Egyptians might have written it:

| Jack and | Jill went up the | hill |
| to get a | pail | of water |

At first glance hieroglyphic writing looks like picture writing. There are certainly a great many pictures in it. And some of the pictures were like those in true picture writing. But Egyptian hieroglyphic writing is not true picture writing. In some cases the pictures stand for sounds, not for the things in the pictures. There are three pictures of a lion in "Jack and Jill," and of course the jingle has nothing to do with lions. Hieroglyphic writing came from picture writing but it was a long way beyond it.

Some of the pictures the Egyptians used stood for syllables. We might write "begun" by drawing a picture of a bee and a picture of a gun. We write words this way in the riddles we call rebuses. Much Egyptian

Egyptian Carving Words on Wall

Chinese Printing

Monk Copying Books on Parchment

Phoenician trading ships carried the alphabet, as well as goods, around the Mediterranean.

writing was rebus writing. A few of the hundreds of pictures stood for simple sounds just as our letters do. The Egyptians also used idea signs. This mark ◯ around a person's name meant "this person is a king or queen."

Egyptian writing was, then, very complicated. There were hundreds of different signs. Moreover, the Egyptians did not always write the same word in the same way. They kept experimenting with ways of writing. No wonder only a few Egyptians in ancient times could read and write!

This is "Jack and Jill" written in cuneiform, another ancient kind of writing:

Jack	and	Jill		went

up	the	hill	to	get

a	pail	of	water

The people who invented this kind of writing lived between the Tigris and the Euphrates rivers. These rivers are not far from the eastern end of the Mediterranean Sea. The Babylonians and the Assyrians were two of the peoples that lived there.

In this region there was much clay along the rivers. Very early the people there learned to use little bricks of soft clay as tablets to write on. They wrote with little sticks of wood. A writer held his stick of wood at a slant and made a mark by pushing it into the soft clay. Each mark was wedge-shaped. "Cuneiform" comes from words meaning "wedge-shaped."

There were thousands of different signs in cuneiform writing. They all came from pictures in the beginning. But it is hard to see pictures in them. Drawing pictures with wedge-shaped marks is not easy. All the thousands of signs in cuneiform writing stood for words or syllables.

One of the most important steps in the story of writing was the invention of the alphabet. It was invented by some group of Semites, peoples who lived at the eastern end of the Mediterranean Sea. They got many of their ideas about writing from the Egyptians, but they worked out a simpler plan. They used just a few more than 20 pictures to stand for the separate sounds in their language. For each sound they used the picture of something with a name that began with that sound. It was as if we should draw a man to stand for the sound of *m* and a dog for the sound of *d*. With their pictures they could write any word they wanted to write.

The Phoenicians, who were Semites, wrote with the semitic alphabet. They were great traders of long ago. They carried the alphabet to the Greeks. By the time the alphabet reached the Greeks the letters did not look like pictures.

The Greeks changed the shapes of many of the letters as they used them. They gave up some letters and added others.

The inventors of the alphabet used it just for writing such things as their names and simple business records and prayers to their gods. The Phoenicians used it for the same kinds of things. But the Greeks used it for many other things, too. They wrote songs and stories and poems and plays.

While the alphabet was on its way to the Greeks it was also traveling in other directions. For instance, it reached the people of India and the Hebrews.

From the Greeks the alphabet traveled to the Romans. They added a few letters and changed the shapes of some. It came down into English, with a few changes along the way, from the Romans. All that we write we write by using only 26 different signs—our 26 letters.

There are other alphabets. There are, moreover, still people who use syllable signs instead of an alphabet. The Chinese, for instance, do.

Many people think that writing is the most important invention in the whole story of civilization. People found it so useful that in time ways were invented of writing by machine. We now have both the typewriter and the printing press.

In writing by hand we sometimes write the letters separately so that they look very much like printed letters. This is called manuscript writing. More often we join the letters together. This is called cursive writing. "Cursive" comes from the Latin word meaning "to run."

Without writing there would be no school books, no story books, no newspapers, no magazines! No letters, no greeting cards! No catalogues! No directions for playing games or putting new toys together! No advertisements and no maps like those we have now! No Declaration of Independence and no Constitution! Much of the wisdom and learning of the past would have been lost if writing had never been invented. Without writing we would be thrown back almost to the days of the cave men. (See ALPHABET; BOOKS AND BOOKBINDING; COMMUNICATION; PAPYRUS; PRINTING.)

EXAMPLES OF ANCIENT HEBREW WRITING

On Parchment

On Limestone Plaque

On Black Basalt

On Pottery

On Rock

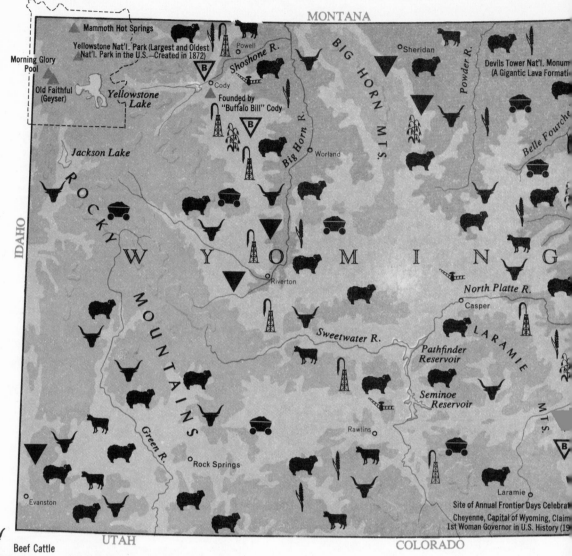

MONTANA

Mammoth Hot Springs
Yellowstone Nat'l. Park (Largest and Oldest
Nat'l. Park in the U.S.—Created in 1872)
Morning Glory Pool
Old Faithful (Geyser)
Yellowstone Lake
Jackson Lake
Powell
Shoshone R.
Cody
Founded by "Buffalo Bill" Cody
BIG HORN MTS.
Sheridan
Powder R.
Devils Tower Nat'l. Monument
(A Gigantic Lava Formation)
Big Horn R.
Worland
Belle Fourche

IDAHO

R O C K Y

W Y O M I N G

M O U N T A I N S

Green R.

Riverton
North Platte R.
Casper
Sweetwater R.
Pathfinder Reservoir
Seminoe Reservoir
LARAMIE MTS.
Rawlins
Rock Springs
Evanston
Laramie
Site of Annual Frontier Days Celebration
Cheyenne, Capital of Wyoming, Claim
1st Woman Governor in U.S. History (19—)

UTAH   COLORADO

Legend

Beef Cattle
Sheep
Dairying
Wheat
Coal
Oil
Natural Gas
Garden Crops
(B) Sugar Beets
Oats
Corn

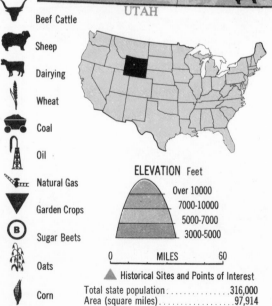

ELEVATION Feet

Over 10000
7000-10000
5000-7000
3000-5000

0   MILES   60

▲ Historical Sites and Points of Interest

Total state population...............316,000
Area (square miles).................97,914

WYOMING In 1868, a new territory was organized in the western part of the United States by taking land from Dakota on the east and from Idaho and Utah on the west and south. Wyoming was a popular name at the time. It is an Indian word meaning "large plains." The name fitted only the eastern part of the new territory. The west was largely mountainous. Nevertheless, the territory was named Wyoming. In 1890, it entered the Union by that name.

The first white settlement in Wyoming was a fur trading post set up in 1834 at what is now Fort Laramie. Two routes followed by pioneers going West passed thru Wyoming. Its dry plains and high moun-

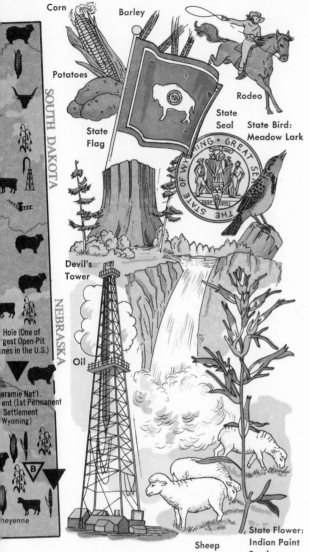

Corn
Barley
Potatoes
Rodeo
State Flag
State Seal
State Bird: Meadow Lark
Devil's Tower
Oil
State Flower: Indian Paint Brush
Sheep

SOUTH DAKOTA
NEBRASKA

Hole (One of gest Open-Pit nes in the U.S.)

aramie Nat'l. ent (1st Permanent Settlement Wyoming)

heyenne

across both Ohio and Indiana to the Illinois line. From north to south it measures 278 miles—about the distance from Chicago to St. Louis. There are about as many people in the whole state as there are in the city of Akron, Ohio. Only two of its 19 cities have as many as 20,000 people; thirteen cities have less than 5,000 each. It is one of the most thinly peopled states. One may travel for miles and miles across Wyoming and see few signs of people.

Today's cattlemen have huge ranches of 10,000 acres or more. Travelers find it hard to pick out the ranches. The ranch buildings are usually grouped in the valleys of streams that flow from the mountains across the plains. Only a small number of the ranchers' cattle are kept on the fenced-in grazing lands of the ranch during the summer. Most of them are taken to the mountains. The ranchers pay the government for the use of the mountain pastures.

Cowboy life is not as thrilling as it used to be. Cowboys like to recall the exciting earlier days by showing their skill in riding horses and roping calves at rodeos. "Frontier Days" at Cheyenne, the capital, is the state's biggest rodeo.

There are some crop farms. Dams have been built which supply power for electricity and water for irrigation. Some farmers on the Great Plains farm successfully without irrigation. The chief crops are hay, sugar beets, beans, and potatoes.

Oil is the biggest industry in the state. Wyoming is not one of the top producing states. But it is in the group producing over 100,000,000 barrels a year. Casper is the oil center. Coal is also mined. Oil and coal lands owned by the state give Wyoming a large school fund.

The third most important work is entertaining tourists. Visitors by the thousands come to enjoy Yellowstone National Park, Grand Teton National Park, the Jackson Hole country, the Big Horn Mountains, and other wonders. Signs such as "Howdy, Stranger" welcome them to Wyoming.

tains were not inviting to the pioneers. Most of them went on in search of more fertile land. Some of them went on to seek gold in California.

In the 1870's Texas cattlemen began driving herds to Wyoming. They found good pasture, and cattle raising began. Cattlemen had many troubles. They overstocked the ranges. Homesteaders claimed land at water holes. Cattle raising, however, is the chief farm work today.

Wyoming is as big and bare as the "Westerns" make it appear. It is one of the largest states, almost a perfect rectangle in shape. From east to west it measures 366 miles—as far as from the Pennsylvania line

THE SWISS FAMILY ROBINSON

Shipwreck

Choosing Site for House

Making Tools

Hunting

WYSS, (VEES) JOHANN RUDOLPH

(1782-1830) Storytelling used to be a much more common art than it is now. In the days before there were many books and before there were movies and television, families provided most of their own entertainment. Telling stories was one of the best-liked forms of family amusement.

Johann David Wyss, a minister in the town of Bern, Switzerland, was the father of four boys. One winter evening, as he and his family sat by the fireplace, he began telling them a story. Night after night he continued, adding more adventures.

The story he told was about a family much like his own. It consisted of a mother, father, and four sons. This imaginary family was shipwrecked and cast up on a tropical island. With no way to get back to civilization, they had to make a life for themselves on their island.

Pastor Wyss must have been a good storyteller, because for years his sons remembered the adventures of the imaginary family. When he was a grown man, one of the sons, Johann Rudolph Wyss, discovered that his father had actually written down the story. It had been hidden away among papers in his father's library. The son changed the story in a few ways and sent it off to a publisher. The story became the book we know today as *The Swiss Family Robinson,* and Johann Rudolph Wyss was listed as the author.

In some ways, *The Swiss Family Robinson* is like *Robinson Crusoe,* which was published earlier. Both tell of people on uninhabited islands who have to learn to make their own houses, tools, and clothing, and to produce their own food.

The Swiss Family Robinson is very popular with children because it tells some marvelous adventures the four boys had as they learned about the ways of nature on their beautiful island. For example, they learned to tame some very unusual pets, among them an eagle, a monkey, an ostrich, a buffalo, and a jackal.

The letter X began as the picture of a fish. The picture is found often in the hieroglyphic writing of the ancient Egyptians. The makers of the first alphabet drew it so that it really looked like a fish (⊲⊐ ⊏▷). The Phoenicians changed it in a curious way. They made it in one of these shapes: ⨎ ⨎ ⧣. The Greeks changed it to this: ☰ . The Romans made it into X as we know it.

The letter stands for several sounds in English. It has a different sound in each of these words: *box, xylophone,* and *anxious.*

XEROPHYTE (ZEE ro fyt) Different kinds of plants are fitted for living in different kinds of places. Some, like cacti and sagebrush, are fitted for living where water is hard to get. Such plants are called xerophytes. This name is from two Greek words. The first two syllables come from the Greek word for "dry"; the last syllable is from the Greek word for "plant."

Some xerophytes have specially good ways of getting what water there is. Many have roots that spread out for a long way or that go deep into the ground. Some xerophytes have specially good ways of keeping the water they get. They may have such small leaves that not much water evaporates from them. They may have no leaves at all. The leaves of some are covered with wax or with hairs. The wax and hairs keep the water in the plants from evaporating. The stems of some xerophytes are so big that they make good storage tanks. The stem of the tree cactus, for example, is a wonderful fluted water tank. The leaves of some xerophytes are thick enough to hold a great deal of water.

Most xerophytes grow in deserts or on dry, rocky cliffs. But some grow in places where there seems to be a great deal of water for plants to use. They grow where salt or acids in the water keep it from soaking into the roots of plants easily. Bogs and salt marshes are such places. Many bog and salt-marsh plants are xerophytes. (See ADAPTATION TO ENVIRONMENT; CACTI.)

XERUS In the big group of rodents there are several small animals that are called ground squirrels. They all look like little squirrels, and they all live in holes in rocks or in burrows in the ground. "Xerus" is the name of one of the kinds of ground squirrels. It lives in South Africa.

This ground squirrel spends a great deal of its time sitting in front of the opening to its burrow. It is like its cousin, the prairie dog, in this way.

African Xerus or Ground Squirrel

XERXES (519 B.C.-465 B.C.) From 485 to 465 B.C. Xerxes was the king of ancient Persia. He is famous chiefly for what he did *not* do.

Darius, the father of Xerxes, had tried to conquer Greece and had failed. Xerxes set out to avenge his father's defeat. With the help of his navy, his army invaded Greece and won an historic victory at the pass of Thermopylae. But shortly afterwards his navy was badly defeated at the Battle of Salamis. The army was left without any supplies and had to withdraw. Xerxes then gave up all hope of conquering Greece.

X RAYS A boy comes to the doctor with a broken arm. The doctor sets it. But is it well set so that the arm will be straight and strong once more? The doctor can soon find out. He can take an X-ray picture.

A baby has swallowed a safety pin. Did it go into his stomach or into his lungs? An X-ray picture will tell.

A man has a toothache. The tooth looks sound, but perhaps it has an abscess at the root. An X-ray picture will help the dentist find out.

Ordinary pictures would not be of any use in cases like these. They are made with light, and light cannot go through arms and chests and teeth. X rays can travel through many substances that light cannot go through at all.

An X-ray picture is really a shadow picture. X rays, for instance, can travel through flesh more easily than through bone. For this reason the bones show up clearly in an X-ray picture of an arm.

Before 1895 no one had X-ray pictures taken because X rays had not yet been discovered. In 1895 a German scientist named Roentgen (RUNT gen) discovered them. X rays had been a nuisance to many scientists before anyone knew that there were such things. For one thing, they were spoiling photographic plates.

For several years before X rays were discovered, scientists had been experimenting by passing a beam of electrons through small tubes called Crookes tubes. They were made of glass and had had most of the air pumped out of them. No one knew that the tubes were giving off, in addition to light, a strange kind of invisible ray. When Roentgen discovered X rays, scientists realized that X rays from their Crookes tubes had been spoiling the plates for their cameras. After X rays were discovered, much better tubes for producing them were made. Modern X-ray tubes send out a powerful stream of these rays.

Instead of taking an X-ray picture, a doctor sometimes has a patient stand or sit in front of a special kind of a screen. The screen is coated with a chemical that glows when X rays strike it. A doctor can often find out what is wrong with a patient by studying the shadow picture of the patient's body on the screen.

X rays do more than help doctors find out what is wrong with their patients. They also help treat some diseases. They are a big help, too, to the makers of such things as airplane motors, ball bearings, rubber tires, and radio tubes. X-ray pictures of these things show up flaws that cannot be seen from the outside.

But X rays can also do great harm. They can cause very dangerous burns if they are not used carefully (See ELECTRICITY; LIGHT; MEDICINE.)

Each bar of the xylophone gives a different sound as it is hit by a hammer.

XYLOPHONE A xylophone is a kind of musical instrument. It is a percussion instrument, just as cymbals and drums are.

The pictures show how a simple xylophone looks. The bars that lie crosswise are made of wood. No two of them are the same length. They get shorter little by little from one end of the xylophone to the other. The player plays the instrument by hitting the bars with small wooden hammers. Each bar gives off a different note of the scale when it is struck. A short bar gives off a higher note than a long bar.

"Xylophone" is a good name for this instrument. It comes from two Greek words that mean "wood" and "sound." The modern xylophone is also called a "marimba." (See PERCUSSION INSTRUMENTS.)

The letter Y is one of the five letters that came from this letter in the Phoenician alphabet: Ч . The Greeks wrote it in two ways (⋏ Y). The Romans borrowed the letter from the Greeks. They wrote it as a rule in this way (∨) but in Greek words they still wrote it with a tail (Y). It stood for the sound of W in some words and of U in others. During the Middle Ages the Y way of writing the letter came to have the sounds it has now.

Y stands for several sounds in English words. It has different sounds in yes, sky, ready, myrtle, and zephyr.

YACHTS (YOTS) The first boats that were called yachts were sailboats built for racing. But now many boats that are driven by engines are also called yachts.

The most famous yacht races are the races for the "America's" Cup. In 1851 the yacht "America" won the cup in a 60-mile race around the Isle of Wight near England. The owners of the "America" were Americans. Yacht owners from England and Canada have tried to win the "America's" Cup. But none has succeeded.

Sir Thomas Lipton, an Englishman, tried five times to win the "America's" Cup. His five yachts were all named "Shamrock." The American yachts that beat the "Shamrocks" were the "Columbia" (twice), "Reliance," "Resolute," and "Enterprise."

Big yachts are very expensive. A yacht large enough to go cruising on the ocean may cost more than a million dollars.

YAK There are not many parts of the world that are less pleasant to live in than the highlands of Tibet. Food is scarce, and the winters are bitterly cold. But in this bleak region the yak is at home.

The yak is a wild ox. The most noticeable thing about a yak is its long hair. Sometimes its hair is so long that it touches the ground. Its heavy coat is a wonderful protection against the cold.

Yaks are great travelers. They have to be to find enough food.

The yak has been tamed. The domestic yak is sometimes called the grunting ox. It gives rich milk, from which butter can be made. The long hair is woven into rope and cloth. When a yak is killed, not even the tail goes to waste. It is dyed red and is used to swish flies away.

But the yak's chief use is as a beast of burden. On steep mountainsides it is as surefooted as a goat. It will walk across glaciers and swim icy streams. Even if it rolls down a steep slope, it will climb right up again. Only one thing makes it hard to use yaks for long journeys in barren regions. They will not eat grain, which could be carried on the journey. They will starve unless they can be brought to a place where there is grass. (See TIBET.)

The long-haired yak is well suited to life in Tibet.

YANKEE To the people of many other countries anyone from the United States is a Yankee. During the War between the States the Southerners called all Northerners Yankees. But the name really belongs only to the people of New England.

During the Revolutionary War the British soldiers called the New England soldiers Yankees. But probably the name had been used before. There are several ideas about where it came from. One is that the word was the Indians' way of saying the French word for English. Another is that it came from an old Scotch word meaning "shrewd." Still another is that it came from a Dutch name and was used only for Dutch settlers at first. No one knows which idea is right. (See NEW ENGLAND.)

YANKEE DOODLE One song that almost every American knows and likes is "Yankee Doodle." The words are foolish, but the tune is a good one.

The song has a long history. A thousand years ago the tune was part of the music of the church in Italy. The Italian people liked it so much that they put other words to it and began singing it in the vineyards as they worked.

It spread from Italy to other parts of Europe. In Holland it was used as a harvest song. In England in Shakespeare's time it was a nursery song. Later in England other sets of words were put to it.

"Yankee Doodle" did not wear an elegant uniform.

The words Americans sing to it now were made up by an English Army doctor at the time of the French and Indian War. He wrote them to make fun of the American soldiers, who were not well trained and did not have good uniforms. But the American soldiers liked both the words and the tune. They began singing the song around their campfires. By the time the Revolutionary War began, "Yankee Doodle" was popular in all the colonies. One day during the war General Gage, a British officer, shouted, "I hope I never have to hear that song again." But at least once more he did have to hear it. His troops were defeated, and he had to surrender. The American troops played "Yankee Doodle" as the British soldiers marched away to go back to England. (See PATRIOTIC SONGS; UNITED STATES HISTORY.)

YEASTS Some plants are too small to be seen without a microscope. Among them are the yeasts. Each yeast plant is a single cell. Although yeasts are tiny, they are important. They help make bread and alcohol.

Yeast plants are almost colorless. They cannot make their food as green plants do. They must have food ready-made. The food they use is sugar. But the sugar must be dissolved in water.

If the temperature is warm and there is plenty of food, yeast plants grow fast. Little bumps grow out on the sides of many of the larger ones. The bumps are really buds, or baby plants. Before long the buds form buds of their own. Sometimes the buds stay together like a string of beads. More often they soon fall apart, and each bud starts forming a new string.

As the yeast plants take in food and grow, they produce materials useless to them. These useless materials are a liquid —alcohol—and a gas—carbon dioxide.

It is the carbon dioxide that the yeast plants throw off which makes bread rise. Bread dough is tough. It will stretch if it is pulled. The little yeast plants in the bread

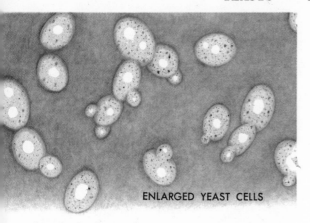
ENLARGED YEAST CELLS

dough feed on the sugar in it and throw off carbon dioxide and alcohol. The carbon dioxide pushes on the bread dough. To make room for the gas the dough stretches. After a time there are little bubbles of gas all through the dough. The dough then takes up much more space. When the bread is baked, the yeast plants are killed by the heat. The alcohol evaporates. The carbon dioxide gas escapes, too. Little spaces are left in the bread where the bubbles of gas were. The bread is "light."

The sugar in fruit juice also serves as food for yeast plants. They use up the sugar, and then the juice becomes sour. Most of the carbon dioxide formed escapes

into the air, but some of it stays in little bubbles in the juice. Most of the alcohol stays in the juice.

The souring of fruit juice is called fermentation. Often people make fruit juice ferment on purpose. They want to change it into an alcoholic drink.

There are yeast plants in the air all the time. If fruit juice is allowed to stand open, yeast plants will probably fall into it. Then, of course, it will turn sour. Yeast plants often make mischief in this way.

"Cakes" of yeast can be bought at grocery stores. Each "cake" contains millions of yeast plants. In the cakes there is not enough sugar or water for the yeasts to grow. Then, too, the cakes are usually kept where it is too cold for yeasts to grow. Yeast cakes make breadmaking easy.

YUGOSLAVIA As the map shows, this new European country is Italy's next-door neighbor to the east. It is in the Balkan Peninsula, which extends southward into the Mediterranean Sea. Between Italy and Yugoslavia is the Adriatic Sea.

In 1914, the world was startled by news of a shot fired in Sarajevo, now a Yugoslav

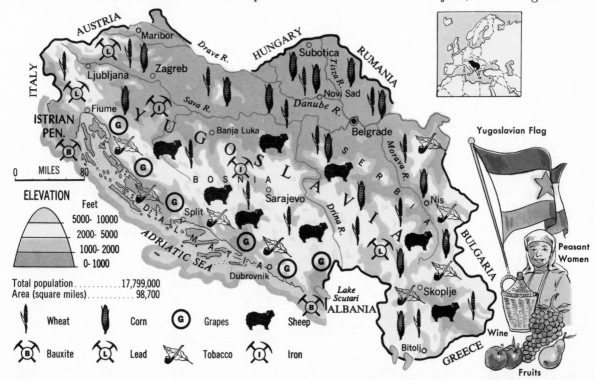

ELEVATION

Feet
5000- 10000
2000- 5000
1000- 2000
0- 1000

Total population..........17,799,000
Area (square miles)..........98,700

Wheat   Corn   (G) Grapes   Sheep

(B) Bauxite   (L) Lead   Tobacco   (I) Iron

Yugoslavian Flag

Peasant Women

Wine

Fruits

city. At that time Sarajevo was the capital of an Austrian province. The shot, fired by a Serbian, killed Archduke Ferdinand of Austria. Austria-Hungary then made war on Serbia. And World War I began.

Serbia was a land of Slavic people. At the end of World War I, a new kingdom was formed by uniting Serbia with another Balkan kingdom and with some neighboring parts of Austria and Hungary. Slavic peoples lived in all those lands. In 1929 this kingdom in southern Europe was named Yugoslavia. The name means "Land of the South Slavs."

That kingdom did not last long, however. It had many internal troubles. And World War II brought great destruction to it. In 1945, after World War II, the present Republic of Yugoslavia was formed. It is a communist republic. But it is not so much shut off from outsiders by a curtain of secrecy as most communist countries are. Its famous first president, Josip Broz, is widely known as "Tito."

Two thirds or more of the Yugoslavs are farmers. As the map suggests, shepherds tend flocks of sheep in upland pastures in the long, wide mountainous part of the country. In the narrow lowland along the Adriatic Sea, crops are much like those along Italy's coasts. Many farmers have vineyards and olive orchards. This lowland is also a vacation land.

In the wide lowland in the northeast, farmers raise so much wheat and corn that northeastern Yugoslavia is often called the country's breadbasket. Except when rainfall is less than usual in the hot summers, there is enough grain for the Yugoslavs, but not for export. The chief export is lumber cut from forests on the sloping land.

Belgrade—the capital, largest city, and chief transportation center—is old. But war destruction there was great and much of the big growing city is new. The second largest city, Zagreb, is in the valley of the Sava River, which flows into the great Danube at Belgrade. There are new factories in some of the towns. And it is hoped that more of the coal, iron, and other minerals in Yugoslavia can soon be used to help increase the number of factories.

YUKON Just east of Alaska is the part of Canada called Yukon Territory. The Klondike, a famous gold-mining region, is in the Yukon. In 1897 and 1898 there was a gold rush to the Klondike. Thousands of people went there to find their fortunes. In 1900 more than $20,000,000 worth of gold was washed out of the streams.

But in a few years all the gold that was easy to get had been taken away. Most of

Men panned for gold in streams.

the people who had come to get rich went back home. Indians and Eskimos were almost the only people left.

Now there are fewer than 13,000 people in a territory that is almost as big as Texas. But there are three times as many as there were in this cold, mountainous, far-off part of Canada in 1940. The Yukon is not as hard to reach as it used to be. The Alaskan Highway cuts across the Yukon Territory for about 600 miles. And every day airlines fly planes to Whitehorse, the capital of the Yukon.

Most of the men there are miners. There are stores of both coal and copper in the Yukon. When supplies of these minerals run low in other parts of the world, there may again be many people in the region. (See CANADA; GOLD.)

The letter Z came from this letter in the Phoenician alphabet: I Some scholars think that it came in the beginning from a picture the ancient Egyptians used in their hieroglyphic writing—the picture of a staff. The Greeks, after the alphabet came to them, changed the letter to look like this (Z). The Romans borrowed it without changing it, and it has come down to us unchanged.

Z stands for two sounds. It has one sound in *zero, zenith, zodiac,* and *buzz.* It has another sound in *azure* and *seizure.*

ZEBRA The zebra is a cousin of the horse. Zebras can be told from horses easily, however, by their stripes. Zebras are always striped. Horses never are.

Once in a while a circus has a team of zebras which are trained to pull a cart. But zebras are very hard to tame and train. Most of them are bad-tempered.

Zebras are found wild in Africa. They run in small herds. People have killed many for meat and hides. But lions are the worst enemies of zebras. It takes about 50 zebras a year to keep one lion well fed. Perhaps even more zebras would be eaten by lions and other meat-eating animals if their stripes did not protect them. A zebra in tall grass or on a dry plain is hard to see. The stripes break up the outline of the animal's body. Zebras themselves eat grass, just as horses do. (See ADAPTATION TO ENVIRONMENT; HORSES.)

ZEBU "Brahman cattle" and "Indian cattle" are other names for zebus. These humped cattle are most common in India, where some of them, usually white ones, are sacred. These sacred cattle wander as they please through Indian villages.

The zebu, or humped ox, is used for work and food.

There are no wild zebus. No one knows how long ago the zebu was tamed. It must have been several thousand years ago. Since that time its wild ancestors have disappeared completely.

Zebus are hardier than most cattle. They are not bothered by some of the diseases many cattle have. Besides they can stand hot, damp weather better than most cattle can. Many zebus have been brought to the United States. They are being crossed with other cattle in the hope of getting beef breeds that will do well in the southern climate. (See CATTLE.)

The zebra roams the plains of Africa in herds.

ZENITH The sky looks like a big bowl turned upside down. The point in the bowl of the sky just above a person or place is called the zenith. Every place has its own zenith. Every person has his own zenith, too. If he points straight up, he is pointing to it. A person's zenith changes as he moves about. Wherever he is, it always looks to him to be the highest point in the whole sky. (See SKY.)

ZERO All the words in the English language are written by using just 26 different letters. In the same way, all the numbers we write, no matter how big they are, are written by using just ten different figures. These figures are 0, 1, 2, 3, 4, 5, 6, 7, 8, and 9. The first of these figures is called "zero."

The zero means "nothing." Perhaps a sign which stands for "nothing" does not seem important. But it is really a great help in writing numbers. We do not need a figure for "ten." We simply use a *1* with a *0* after it. A *1* with two zeros stands for "one hundred." Adding another zero changes "one hundred" to "one thousand." Adding three more zeros changes "one thousand" to "one million."

Zero is a place holder. It makes the other figures mean what we want them to mean by keeping them in their proper places. To write a number like "fifty million, two hundred thousand, two hundred fifty-four" without using zeros we would have to have special figures for tens, hundreds, thousands, and millions. How much simpler it is to write it like this: 50,200,254!

Zero was a great invention. It is not as old an invention as most people would guess. Probably it was not invented much more than 1,000 years ago. No one knows where it was invented or who invented it. All we can be sure of is that zero was being used in both India and Arabia shortly before the year 900. (See MATHEMATICS; NUMBERS.)

ZINC Most people, at least in the United States, have seen a great deal of the metal called zinc. But probably some of them may not know that they have. They may not know that when they see a bucket or a tub or a roof made of galvanized iron they are really seeing zinc. But it is true, for galvanized iron is iron with a coating of zinc. The iron in a piece of galvanized iron does not show. Anyone who has ever seen a flashlight battery has seen zinc, too. This is because the "can" of each little dry cell in a flashlight battery and of every other dry cell is made of zinc.

Zinc is not a pretty metal. It does not take a high polish. But no other metal works so well in dry cells. And it is very useful as a coating for iron because it does not rust. A solid sheet of zinc roofing no thicker than the cover of this book would last, it is said, several hundred years. Galvanized iron does not last nearly so long, but it lasts much longer than plain sheet iron.

Zinc is never found pure. It is always joined with other materials. There are several kinds of zinc ore. Not one gives up its zinc easily. It is no wonder that people knew about some of the other metals long before they knew about zinc.

Brass is made of zinc and copper. The ancient Romans without knowing about zinc made brass. They made it out of zinc ore and copper. They had no idea what it was in the ore that made the copper into a beautiful yellowish metal.

About 400 years ago Portuguese traders began bringing zinc back from China and India. Probably the Chinese and Hindus had been getting zinc from ore for centuries. In time the people of Europe learned how to get zinc from its ores. Today the United States produces more zinc than any other country in the world.

Nations at war need huge amounts of zinc. A great deal is needed for making brass for cartridges and shell cases. Much is needed, too, for making galvanized iron for camp equipment. Some compounds of

ORES OF ZINC

zinc, substances in which zinc is joined with other materials, are very useful. Some of them are used in house paints because they last a long time and cover up well what is under them. Some are used in paper and white-walled tires. Their good covering power makes them useful in face powders. And some zinc compounds are useful for their healing powers. Zinc ointment is found in many home medicine chests. (See COMPOUNDS; COPPER; METALS.)

GREEK SIGNS OF THE ZODIAC

Aries

Taurus

Leo

Virgo

Sagittarius

Capricornus

Gemini

Libra

Aquarius

Cancer

Scorpius

Pisces

ZODIAC The word "zodiac" means "circle of animals." But there are no real animals in the zodiac. The zodiac animals are constellations, or groups of stars, that were named for various animals by the people of long ago. As centuries passed, some of these constellations came to be thought of as pictures of people. One, Libra, came to be thought of as a pair of scales.

The 12 constellations of the zodiac are along the path in the heavens which the sun, to watchers on the earth, appears to follow. The sun seems to stay in each of these constellations for about a month. Of course, the sun does not really move from one constellation to another. It seems to move because the earth travels once around the sun every year.

The list below names the constellations of the zodiac. In late March the sun is in the constellation of Aries, the Ram. If we could see stars in the daytime we would see Aries rise, move across the sky, and set with the sun. A month later the sun is in Taurus, the Bull, and so on. The next March it is back in Aries again.

Aries—The Ram	Libra—The Balance
Taurus—The Bull	Scorpius—The Scorpion
Gemini—The Twins	Sagittarius—The Archer
Cancer—The Crab	Capricornus—The Goat
Leo—The Lion	Aquarius—The Water Carrier
Virgo—The Virgin	Pisces—The Fishes

ZOOLOGY The science of zoology is the study of animals. There are about a million different kinds of animals, and there are many, many things to be learned about them. Here are some of the questions the scientists who study animals have been trying to answer:

Which animals are closely related?

How are different animals built?

How do the various kinds of animals keep themselves alive?

In what parts of the world are the different kinds of animals found?

Snakes can be kept in homemade cages while their habits are being studied.

Animals may take their own pictures by means of a "camera trap."

Zebra

Kangaroo

Lion

How are they fitted for living in the places where they do?

Why do animals behave as they do?

How do animals produce offspring?

What kinds of diseases do different kinds of animals have?

How can we best take care of the animals we raise?

How can we develop new and better kinds of animals?

How have the animals of today come from those of long ago?

Zoology has many branches. We can easily understand why it has when we realize how many things there are to be found out about animals.

A scientist who studies animals is called a zoologist. No zoologist ever tries to learn everything there is to know about animals. He chooses the animals or the problems that interest him most. One zoologist may spend his whole life studying snails while another one studies some animal disease. There are enough animals and enough problems to go around. (See ADAPTATION TO ENVIRONMENT; ANIMAL BABIES; ANIMAL BREEDING; ANIMAL KINGDOM; CARNIVOROUS ANIMALS; LIFE THROUGH THE AGES; OMNIVOROUS ANIMALS.)

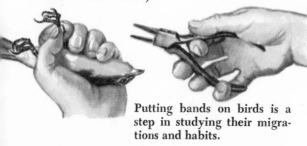

Putting bands on birds is a step in studying their migrations and habits.

Scientists have learned much about animals of the past and present by studying bones.

ZOOS Where would one go to see a giraffe, a polar bear, and an ostrich? To the zoo, of course. The word "zoo" comes from a Greek word for "animal." Sometimes zoos are called "zoological gardens."

In a zoo of today there are animals from many different parts of the world. A tiger from India may be next to a lion from Africa or a panther from Mexico. In a few minutes in a zoo, a person can see animals that he would have to travel thousands of miles to see in their native homes.

In the newer zoos, the places for the animals are as nearly like their native homes as possible. Many of the animals are out in the open all the time.

It is not easy to make animals from many different parts of the world comfortable in any one place. In its native home a polar bear may live on ice all the year round. Spider monkeys come from hot lands where there is no snow. The keepers at the zoo do all that they can to keep the polar bears cool and the monkeys warm.

Feeding all the animals in a zoo is not easy, either. The elephants must have hay, and lots of it. But the tigers could not live on a diet of hay. Nothing but meat will do for them. The seals must have fresh fish, while the monkeys need fresh fruit and vegetables. A hundred kinds of food may be needed for all the animals in a zoo. A big zoo buys tons of beef, bread, fish, hay, and grain for its animals every year. It also buys such things as bananas, raisins, oranges, eggs, dried milk, dried flies, and ground grasshoppers.

Sometimes coaxing an animal to eat is a problem. The big snakes are about as much trouble to feed as any animals in a zoo. A boa constrictor may have to have its food pushed down its throat.

Taking care of animals that are sick or hurt is another big problem at a zoo. It is not easy to pull a bad tooth for a lion with a toothache, or to trim the toenails of an elephant whose feet hurt, or to take care of a gorilla with pneumonia.

The idea of a zoo is not new. The oldest zoo anyone knows about was in ancient Assyria. Here in the city now called Nimrud the kings of Assyria had a great zoo 2,800 years ago. Records tell that in this zoo there were "15 mighty lions, and 50 cubs for the cages in the palace." There were dolphins, wild bulls, wild asses, gazelles, stags, panthers, and monkeys, too.

C

Matisse, Henri 11-1048
Mayas 10-868
empire 7-652; Guatemala 3-286; quetzal 12-1152
Mayflower 10-870
Pilgrims 12-1100
Mazarin, Jules, Cardinal 14-1302
McCormick, Cyrus 6-510, 8-719, 15-1404
McHenry, Fort 2-144
McKinley, William 12-1132
Measles 10-870
Meat and Meat-Packing 10-870
Chicago 4-299; food 6-536; Omaha 11-966; salt 13-1215; vitamins15-1436
Medals see **Decorations of Honor**
Medieval Life
cathedrals 3-272; dark ages 5-394; middle ages 10-888
Medicine 10-872
alcohol 1-34; antiseptics 1-69; blood 2-191; body, human 3-197; dentistry 5-412; drugs 5-433; experiments 6-497; Gorgas, W. 11-1051; Harvey, W. 7-626; health 7-630; herbs 7-639; hospitals 7-668; infrared rays 8-708; iodine 8-721; Jenner 8-743; Linnaeus, C. 9-814; malaria 9-842; Nightingale, Florence 11-995; Pasteur 12-1064; penicillin 10-910, 12-1072; physiology 12-1096; psychology 12-1142; Reed 13-1170; sulfur 14-1314; veterinary medicine 15-1426; X rays 16-1504
Mediterranean Sea 10-874
Adriatic Sea 16-1507; Bosporus 2-190, 3-207; Crete 4-372; Dardanelles 5-393; Gibraltar 14-1307; Marco Polo 2-109, 9-854; Near East 11-964; Nile River 11-996, 13-1185; Phoenicians 12-1090; Suez Canal 13-1169, 14-1312
Melville, Herman 1-50
Memorial Day 10-875
Mendel, Gregor 10-875 7-640
Mendelssohn, Felix 4-346
Menotti, Gian-Carlo 11-1029
Mercury 12-1108, 13-1200
Mercury 10-876
barometers 2-151; elements 5-460; liquid 10-877; liquid air 9-816; metals 10-877; mirrors 10-899; thermometers 15-1350
Mergenthaler, Ottmar 8-718, 12-1136
Meridian see **Latitude and Longitude**
Mermaids 10-876
Mesmerism 8-682
Mesopotamia 2-131, 8-725
Mesozoic Era 5-441
Metals 10-877
alloys 1-42; aluminum 1-46; bronze 3-219; chromium 4-310; copper 4-364; electrical conductors 7-633; germanium 15-1366; gold 7-590; iron and steel 8-727; lead 9-785; mercury 10-876; mirrors 10-899; nickel 11-994; platinum 12-1118; radium 13-1161; silver 14-1252; tin 15-1357; titanium 15-1358; uranium 15-1413; vanadium 12-1082; zinc 16-1511
Meteorology 10-878
U.S. Weather Bureau 15-1408
Meteors and Meteorites 10-878
satellites 13-1218; size 14-1289
Metternich, Prince Klemens von 14-1302
Mexico 10-880
Cortés 4-368; jumping beans 8-754; Mayas 10-868; Mexico City 10-881; Mt. Orizaba 10-938; Mt. Popocatepetl 10-938; Parícutin 12-1059; quetzal 12-1152; Rivera, Diego 11-1046; U.N. member 15-1388; volcanoes 15-1440
Mexico City 4-315, 10-881
Mica 10-892; 13-1193
Mice see **Rodents**
Michelangelo 10-882
painters and paintings 11-1048; Raphael 13-1167; Renaissance 7-654, 13-1174; sculptor 13-1229
Michigan 10-884
Grand Rapids 6-557; Mackinac Strait 14-1307; United States 15-1390

Microfilm 10-886
camera 3-244; photography 12-1092
Microscope 10-886
chalk 4-291; compound 8-718; disease germs 5-423; Leeuwenhoek 9-791, 10-873; lenses 9-795; mirrors 10-899; plankton 12-1110; protozoa 12-1141; salt 13-1215
Midas 10-888
Middle Ages 10-888
advertising 1-8; alchemy 1-34, 7-590; armor 1-94; black death 2-190; castles 3-270; cathedrals 3-272; chemistry 1-34; Christianity 4-308; cities 4-315; crusades 4-376, 7-661; dark ages 5-394; fairs 6-504; hawking 7-629; history 7-646; Holy Land 7-661; horses 7-666; jesters 8-745; justice 8-756; knighthood 6-526, 8-764; Latin 5-476, 9-781; medicine 10-872; money-lenders 2-148; monks 3-203, 7-668, 9-799, 10-921; mosaics 10-930; numbers 10-867; roads 13-1186; Roman Catholic Church 13-1199; schools 13-1224; soap 14-1269; spices 14-1292; stained glass 7-588; trade 15-1365; troubadours 15-1374; weapons 16-1459
Milk 10-890
butter 3-227; cheese 4-293; cream 3-287; dairying 5-387; food 6-536; ice cream 8-685
Milky Way 10-891
Millet, Jean François 11-1048
Milne, A. A. 5-478
Milton, John 5-478
Minerals 10-892
alloys 1-42; asbestos 2-103; calcium 10-890; coal 4-328; corundum 6-568; crystals 4-379; gems 6-567; gold 7-590; granite 13-1193; iron and steel 8-727; jade 8-739; mineralogy 6-571; mines and mining 10-894; nickel 11-994; ocean water 11-1018; ochers 11-1044; petrified wood 12-1083; pitchblende 15-1413; quartz 12-1150; silver 14-1252
Mines and Mining 10-894
coal 4-329; copper 4-364, 10-923; diamond 5-417; explosives 6-500; gold 7-590; industries 8-707; largest silver in U.S. 8-689; lung disease 5-425; nickel 11-994; salt 13-1215; sulfur 14-1314; vanadium 12-1082
Mink 6-558, 11-1040
Minnesota 10-896
Minstrels see **Troubadours**
Mirage 10-898
Mirrors 10-898
kaleidoscope 8-757; light 9-807; periscope 12-1078; telescope 14-1334
Missiles, Guided 13-1191
Missions 10-899
Mississippi 10-900
United States 15-1390
Mississippi River 10-902
conservation 4-356; delta 5-408; erosion 6-483; Gulf of Mexico 7-613, 13-1185, 14-1273; La Salle 9-781; Marquette and Joliet 9-857
Missouri 10-904
Pony Express 12-1126; rainfall record 13-1165; Twain, Mark 15-1381; United States 15-1390
Mistletoe 10-906
decoration 4-310; parasite 11-1056
Modern Art 10-906
Mohair 7-589
Mohammed 10-908
Islam 8-732; Jerusalem 8-744; religious founder 2-107, 7-652
Molds 10-910
Molecules 10-911
Moles and Shrews 10-912
Mollusks 10-913
clams 4-318; octopus 11-1019; oyster 11-1042; shellfish 13-1242; snails 14-1265; squids 14-1296
Molybdenum 5-460; 8-729

Monaco 10-914
Monarchy 10-914
governments 7-594
Monasteries see **Monks and Monasteries**
Monet, Claude 11-1048
Money 10-915
copper coins 3-219, 4-364; gold 7-590; salt 13-1215; shells 13-1243; silver coins 14-1252; U.S. Constitution 15-1398; U.S. Government 7-596
Mongolia 10-918
Mongoose 10-919
Monitor and the Merrimac 10-919
Monkeys 10-920
galagos 6-559; lemurs 2-128; nails 10-951; tarsiers 14-1327; uakari 15-1383
Monks and Monasteries 10-921
Mendel, Gregor 10-875; Middle Ages 3-203, 7-668; Roman Catholic Church 13-1199
Monroe, James 12-1132, 14-1302; Monroe Doctrine 15-1405; White House 16-1475
Montana 10-922
National Parks 10-958
Monteverdi, Claudio 11-1029
Montreal 10-924
Canada 3-248; La Salle 9-781
Moon 10-925
eclipses 5-444; Galileo 6-561; radar waves 13-1158; tides 15-1352
Moors 10-927
Alhambra 1-40; Spain 7-654
Mormons 10-928
Utah 15-1416
Morocco 14-1307
Morse, Samuel Finley Breese 10-929
telegraph 7-655, 8-719, 14-1331
Morton, William T. 10-873
Mosaic 10-930
Moscow 10-930
Leningrad 9-794; Napoleon 10-955; population 4-315; U.S.S.R. 15-1385
Moslems
Islam 8-732; Mohammed 10-908; religions of the world 13-1172
Mosques
Damascus 5-389; Islam 8-732; Mohammed 10-909
Mosquitoes 10-931
animal kingdom 1-65; anopheles 9-842; disease carriers 8-711, 11-1051; Finley 10-873; insects 8-713; larva 9-780; Reed 13-1170
Moss 10-932
Mother Goose 10-932
Moths see **Butterflies and Moths**
Motion Pictures 10-934
communication 4-344; copyright 4-365; Edison 5-447; Hollywood 3-241; Los Angeles 9-827; theaters 15-1349
Motorcycles see **Bicycles and Motorcycles**
Mound Builders 10-936
Mountains 10-937
Alps 1-45; Andes 1-58; Apennines 8-738, 13-1217; Appalachians 1-72; earth history 5-439; Harz Mountains 3-254; Himalayas 7-643, 8-697; Khyber Pass 11-1050; national parks 10-958; Pikes Peak 12-1099; plateaus 12-1118; Rockies 13-1195; Sierra Madre 10-881; Sugar Loaf 13-1182; timber line 15-1353; tunnels 15-1375; volcanoes 15-1439; waterfalls 16-1454
Mount Aconcagua 10-938, 15-1440
Mount Cotopaxi 10-938, 15-1440
Mount Elbert 10-938
Mount Elborus 10-938
Mount Erebus 1-67, 10-938, 15-1440
Mount Etna 15-1440
Mount Everest 7-643, 10-938
Mount Fuji 10-938, 15-1440
Mount Godwin Austen 10-938
Mount Greylock 10-938
Mount Hood 10-938, 15-1440
Mount Ida 4-372

O

Oaks 11-1017
furniture 6-557; long moss 9-826;
wood 16-1487
Oasis 5-389, 5-414
Oats 4-366, 7-600
Obelisk 11-1018
Obsidian 7-587, 13-1192
Ocean Liners see Ships
Oceans 11-1018
Arctic 1-84; Atlantic 2-114; Gulf
Stream 7-614; harbors 7-622; Indian
8-700; International Date Line 8-716;
islands 8-733; latitude and longitude
9-782; mirages 10-898; North Sea
11-1008; Pacific 10-952, 11-1043;
tides 15-1352
Ocelot 3-274
Octavius Caesar see Caesars 3-233
Octopus 11-1019
Ohio 11-1020
corn belt 4-367; maple sugar 9-851
Oil
Arkansas 1-90; Asia 2-107; diatoms
5-417; fuel oil 6-555; heating 7-634;
Iraq 8-725; Near East 11-965;
Oklahoma 11-1022; Pennsylvania
12-1074; perfumes 12-1077;
petroleum 12-1084; Texas 14-1342;
Venezuela 15-1421
Oilcloth see Linoleum and Oilcloth
Oklahoma 11-1022
Platt National Park 10-958
Old Glory 11-1024
flags 6-526
"Old Ironsides" 11-1024
Olds, R. E. 2-125
Oleomargarine 11-1025
Olives 11-1025
Olympic crown 11-1026
Olympic Games 11-1026
basketball 2-157; diving 5-426;
games and sports 6-565; Greeks
2-113, 6-565, 7-605; ice skating
8-687; olive crown 11-1025; swim-
ming 14-1320; winter sports 16-1483
Omnivorous Animals 11-1027
Opera 11-1028
ballet 2-141; composers 4-346;
music 10-945; orchestra 11-1034
Operettas 11-1030
Gilbert and Sullivan 7-582
Opossums 12-1130
Optical Illusions 11-1032
mirage 10-898
Oracles 11-1033
Orchestra 11-1034
composers 4-346; drums 5-433;
Haydn 7-629; music 10-945; musical
instruments 10-946; opera 11-1028;
percussion instruments 12-1076;
stringed instruments 10-947, 14-1308;
wind instruments 16-1480
Orchids 11-1035
epiphytes 5-480; jungles 8-755
Oregon 11-1036
Crater Lake National Park 10-958;
Mt. Hood 10-938, 15-1440
Oregon Trail 12-1104
Ores
iron 8-727; lead 9-785; minerals
10-892; nickel 11-994; zinc 16-1511
Organ 11-1038
Osaka 11-1039
Japan 8-740
Osmium see Metals 10-877
Ostrich 11-1039
animal kingdom 1-65; birds 2-182
Otis, Elisha G. 8-718
Otter 11-1040
Owls 11-1040
birds of prey 2-186
Oxygen 11-1041
air 1-19, 7-600; breathing 3-215;
element 3-197, 5-460; liquid air
9-816; molecules 10-911; plants 1-76;
Priestley 12-1134; water 16-1452
Oysters 11-1042
mollusks 10-913; pearls 12-1069

P

Pacific Ocean 11-1043
Balboa 2-140; International Date
Line 8-716; islands in 8-733, 15-1394;
Magellan strait 14-1307; oceans
11-1018; Panama Canal 11-1051;
San Francisco Bay 14-1307;
typhoons 14-1305
Pagoda 11-1044
Paint 11-1044
chemistry 4-297; lead compounds
9-785; radium 13-1161; turpentine
15-1378; zinc 16-1511
Painted Desert 11-1045
Painters and Paintings 11-1046
cave men 3-278, 7-646; Giotto 7-584;
Madonna 9-835; Michelangelo
10-882; modern art 10-906; mosaic
10-930; Raphael 13-1166; Rembrandt
13-1173; Renaissance 7-654
13-1174; Renoir 13-1175; sculpture
13-1228; Vinci, Leonardo da 15-1432
Pakistan 3-218, 11-1050
Paleontology 11-1051
fossils 6-544; geology 6-571
Paleozoic Era 5-441
Palestine
Dead Sea 5-400; Hebrews 7-648;
Israel 8-734; Roman Empire 7-661
Palladium see Metals 10-877
Palm
coconut 4-330; Doom palm 7-583
Panama 3-284, 15-1388
Panama Canal 11-1051
canals 3-253; Canal Zone 3-285
Paper 11-1052
Chinese 7-651, 9-855; lumbering
9-830; newspapers 11-986; papyrus
12-1090; wood pulp 15-1370
Papyrus 11-1054
books 3-202, 12-1090; plant 3-202,
5-449, 16-1497; scrolls 1-37, 9-798
Parachute 11-1054
Blanchard 8-719; nylon 11-1016
Paraguay 11-1055
South America 14-1282; U.N. 15-1388
Parakeets see Parrots and Parakeets
Paramecium 12-1141
Parasites 11-1056
malaria 9-842; mistletoe 10-906;
tapeworms and hookworms 16-1494
Parchment 3-203, 9-799
Pare, Ambroise 10-873
Parícutin 12-1059, **15-1440**
Paris 12-1060
Eiffel Tower 5-452; France 6-549;
Napoleon 10-954; Versailles 6-567
Parrots and Parakeets 12-1062
jungles 8-755; oldest known 1-17;
pets 12-1086; voices 15-1438
Partnerships Among Living Things
12-1062
Passenger Pigeon 12-1064
pigeons 12-1097
Passion Play 12-1064
Pasteur, Louis 12-1064
disease germs 1-69, 6-497, 10-873
Patents 12-1066
governments 7-596; inventions 8-717
Patriotic Songs 12-1067
Yankee Doodle 16-1506
Patriots 12-1068
Boone, D. 3-206; Douglas, S. A.
5-432; Franklin, B. 6-550; Hale, N.
7-619; Henry, P.,7-637; Jefferson, T.
8-741; Jones, J. P. 8-753; Lafayette
9-772; Lee, R. E. 9-790; Lincoln, A.
9-810; presidents 12-1132; Revere, P.
13-1178; Roosevelt, F. D. 13-1206;
Smith, J. 14-1262; statesmen
14-1302; Washington, G. 16-1446;
Webster, D. 16-1463
Peanuts 3-268, 9-792
Pearl Harbor 12-1069
Hawaii 7-627; World War II 16-1493
Pearls 12-1069
gems 6-569; oysters 11-1042
Peary, Robert E. 12-1070
explorer 6-499; North Pole 11-1008

Peat 12-1070
bog mosses 10-932; fuel 6-555, 8-726
Pebbles 12-1071
Peiping 4-302, 4-315
Pelicans 3-264, 16-1453
Penguins 12-1072
Penicillin 12-1072
discovery 1-69, 10-873; drug 5-433
Peninsula 12-1073
Penn, William 12-1073
Pennsylvania 12-1074; Philadelphia
12-1088; Quakers 12-1148
Pennsylvania 12-1074
Mason and Dixon's Line 9-861;
Penn, William 12-1073; Philadelphia
12-1088; Quakers 12-1148
Pepusch, John Christopher 11-1031
Percussion Instruments 12-1076
bands 2-146; musical instruments
10-946; orchestra 11-1034; piano
12-1096; xylophone 16-1504
Perfumes 12-1077
ambergris 1-48; coal tar 4-330;
flowers 6-565; herbs 7-639
Periscope 12-1078
mirrors 10-899; submarine 14-1311
Perkins, Jacob 8-719
Perón, Juan D. 1-86, 5-418
Perpetual Motion 12-1078
Persia 12-1078
Alexander the Great 1-36; Asia 2-107;
Babylonia 8-750; Egypt 7-649; Iran
8-724; Xerxes 15-1408, 16-1503
Peru 12-1082
Bolívar 3-200; Incas 8-693; Mt. Misti
15-1440; Pizarro 12-1129; South
America 14-1282; Titicaca 15-1358;
U.N. 15-1388; vicuñas 15-1428
Petrified Wood 12-1083
Petrograd see **Leningrad** 9-795
Petroleum 12-1084
butadiene 13-1209; fibers 6-515; fuel
6-555; Texas production 14-1342
Pets 12-1086
cats 3-274; dogs 5-428; goldfish
7-592; hamsters 7-620; parrots and
parakeets 12-1062; rabbits 13-1155;
tropical fish 15-1373
Pewter
lead 9-785; tin 15-1357
Phidias
Greece 7-607; sculpture 13-1229;
seven wonders of the world 13-1236
Philadelphia 12-1088
circus 4-312; Continental Congress
2-100, 5-401; Independence Hall
15-1398; Liberty Bell 9-798; mint
10-916; Penn, William 12-1073; Pennsylvania 12-1074; U.S. capital 11-991
Philippines, Republic of the 12-1089
Magellan 9-836; rainfall record
13-1165; U.N. member 15-1388;
U.S. former possession 15-1405
Philosophy
Aristotle 1-87; Diogenes 5-422;
Socrates 14-1271
Phoenicians 12-1090
alphabet 1-43, 7-649, 15-1357,
16-1498; Carthage 7-649; Crete
4-374; Greece 7-605; Mediterranean
10-874; traders 5-436, 16-1498
Phonograph 12-1091
Edison 5-447; music boxes 10-947
Phosphorus 12-1092
elements 3-197, 5-460; matches 9-864
Photography 12-1092
camera 3-244; Daguerre 8-719;
daguerreotype 5-387; Eastman 8-718;
infrared rays 8-708; Lippman 8-719;
microfilm 10-886; X rays 16-1504
Photosynthesis see Plant Factories
Physics 12-1095
Archimedes 1-80; capillary attraction
3-259; centrifugal force 3-287; cosmic
rays 4-369; echo 5-444; Einstein, A.
5-452; electricity 5-454; electronics
5-458; energy 5-465; engineering
13-1226; Faraday 6-507; Franklin,B.
6-550; friction 6-551; Galileo 6-560;

THE GOLDEN BOOK ENCYCLOPEDIA

CONTAINS THE FOLLOWING VOLUMES

CONTRIBUTING ARTISTS

Dot and Sy Barlowe • Cornelius De Witt • E. Joseph Dreany • Bruno Frost
James Gordon Irving • Beth and Joe Krush • Harry Lazarus • Andre LeBlanc
H. Charles McBarron • Denny McMains • Harry McNaught
Ray Perlman • John Polgreen • Evelyn Urbanowich

Pauline Batchelder Adams • George Avison • Barry Bart • Ernie Barth • Charles Bellow
Eric Bender • Juanita Bennett • Merrit Berger • Robert D. Bezucha • William Bolin
Thelma Bowie • Matilda Breuer • S. Syd Brown • Peter Buchard • Louise Fulton Bush
Jim Caraway • Nino Carbe • Sam Citron • Gordon Clifton • Mel Crawford • Robert Doremus
Harry Daugherty • Rachel Taft Dixon • Olive Earle • Sydney F. Fletcher • F. Beaumont Fox
Rudolf Freund • Tibor Gergely • Douglas Gorsline • Hamilton Greene • Gerald Gregg
Marjorie Hartwell • Hans H. Helweg • Janice Holland • W. Ben Hunt
Arch and Miriam Hurford • Harper Johnson • Norman Jonsson • Matthew Kalmenoff
Janet Robson Kennedy • Paul Kinnear • Olga Kucera • Walter Kumme • John Leone
Kenneth E. Lowman • John Alan Maxwell • Jean McCammack • Shane Miller • Stina Nagel
Elizabeth Newhall • Gregory Orloff • Raymond Pease • Alice and Martin Provensen
Jerry Robinson • Feodor Rojankovsky • Roki • Mary Royt • Arnold W. Ryan
Arthur Sanford • Sam Savitts • William Sayles • Al Schmidt • Edwin Schmidt
Frederick E. Seyfarth • Robert Sherman • George Solonewitsch • Lionel Stern
Norton Stewart • Valerie Swenson • Gustaf Tenggren • William Thompson • Felix Traugott
Eileen Fox Vaughn • Herschel Wartik • Robert Weisman • Garth Williams

MAPS BY

Vincent Kotschar   Jean Paul Tremblay
Carol Vinall   Frederic Lorenzen
Rudolf von Siegl   Francis Barkoczy

COVER ARTISTS

Ned Seidler • Ken Davies • Don Moss